Lecture Notes in Computer Science   13736

More information about this series at https://link.springer.com/bookseries/558

Yuchao Zhang · Liang-Jie Zhang (Eds.)

Web Services – ICWS 2022

29th International Conference
Held as Part of the Services Conference Federation, SCF 2022
Honolulu, HI, USA, December 10–14, 2022
Proceedings

 Springer

Editors
Yuchao Zhang
Beijing University of Posts
and Telecommunications
Beijing, China

Liang-Jie Zhang (ID)
Kingdee International Software
Group Co., Ltd.
Shenzhen, China

ISSN 0302-9743   ISSN 1611-3349 (electronic)
Lecture Notes in Computer Science
ISBN 978-3-031-23578-8   ISBN 978-3-031-23579-5 (eBook)
https://doi.org/10.1007/978-3-031-23579-5

This Springer imprint is published by the registered company Springer Nature Switzerland AG
The registered company address is: Gewerbestrasse 11, 6330 Cham, Switzerland

Preface

The 2022 International Conference on Web Services (ICWS) was an international forum for both researchers and industry practitioners to exchange the latest fundamental advances in the state of the art and practice of Web-based services, to identify emerging research topics, and to define the future of Web-based services. All topics regarding Internet/Web services lifecycle study and management aligned with the theme of ICWS.

ICWS 2022 was one of the events of the Services Conference Federation event (SCF 2022), which had the following 10 collocated service-oriented sister conferences: the International Conference on Web Services (ICWS 2022), the International Conference on Cloud Computing (CLOUD 2022), the International Conference on Services Computing (SCC 2022), the International Conference on Big Data (BigData 2022), the International Conference on AI & Mobile Services (AIMS 2022), the International Conference on Metaverse (METAVERSE 2022), the International Conference on Internet of Things (ICIOT 2022), the International Conference on Cognitive Computing (ICCC 2022), the International Conference on Edge Computing (EDGE 2022), and the International Conference on Blockchain (ICBC 2022).

This volume presents the papers accepted at ICWS 2022. Each paper was reviewed by three independent members of the Program Committee. After carefully evaluating their originality and quality, we accepted 9 papers.

We are pleased to thank the authors whose submissions and participation made this conference possible. We also want to express our thanks to the Organizing Committee and Program Committee members, for their dedication in helping to organize the conference and review the submissions. We owe special thanks to the keynote speakers for their impressive talks.

Finally, we would like to thank operations team members Yishuang Ning, Sheng He and Jing Zeng, for their excellent work in organizing this conference.

December 2022

Yuchao Zhang
Liang-Jie Zhang

Organization

Services Conference Federation (SCF 2022)

General Chairs

Ali Arsanjani   Google, USA
Wu Chou   Essenlix, USA

Coordinating Program Chair

Liang-Jie Zhang   Kingdee International Software Group, China

CFO and International Affairs Chair

Min Luo   Georgia Tech, USA

Operation Committee

Jing Zeng   China Gridcom, China
Yishuang Ning   Tsinghua University, China
Sheng He   Tsinghua University, China

Steering Committee

Calton Pu   Georgia Tech, USA
Liang-Jie Zhang   Kingdee International Software Group, China

ICWS 2022

Program Chair

Yuchao Zhang   Beijing University of Posts and
                         Telecommunications, China

Program Committee

Marios-Eleftherios Fokaefs   Polytechnique Montréal, Canada
Keke Gai   Beijing Institute of Technology, China
Heba Ismail   United Arab Emirates University, UAE
Hyuk-Yoon Kwon   Seoul National University of Science &
                             Technology, South Korea

Zakaria Maamar   Zayed University, UAE
Dhaval Patel   IBM T.J. Watson Research Center, USA
Young-Kyoon Suh   Kyungpook National University, South Korea
Haibo Zhang   University of Otago, New Zealand
Rui Zhang   Institute of Information Engineering, Chinese
                        Academy of Sciences, China

Services Society

The Services Society (S2) is a non-profit professional organization that was created to promote worldwide research and technical collaboration in services innovations among academia and industrial professionals. Its members are volunteers from industry and academia with common interests. S2 is registered in the USA as a "501(c) organization", which means that it is an American tax-exempt nonprofit organization. S2 collaborates with other professional organizations to sponsor or co-sponsor conferences and to promote an effective services curriculum in colleges and universities. S2 initiates and promotes a "Services University" program worldwide to bridge the gap between industrial needs and university instruction.

The Services Society has formed Special Interest Groups (SIGs) to support technology- and domain-specific professional activities:

- Special Interest Group on Web Services (SIG-WS)
- Special Interest Group on Services Computing (SIG-SC)
- Special Interest Group on Services Industry (SIG-SI)
- Special Interest Group on Big Data (SIG-BD)
- Special Interest Group on Cloud Computing (SIG-CLOUD)
- Special Interest Group on Artificial Intelligence (SIG-AI)
- Special Interest Group on Edge Computing (SIG-EC)
- Special Interest Group on Cognitive Computing (SIG-CC)
- Special Interest Group on Blockchain (SIG-BC)
- Special Interest Group on Internet of Things (SIG-IOT)
- Special Interest Group on Metaverse (SIG-Metaverse)

Services Conference Federation (SCF)

As the founding member of SCF, the first International Conference on Web Services (ICWS) was held in June 2003 in Las Vegas, USA. The First International Conference on Web Services - Europe 2003 (ICWS-Europe'03) was held in Germany in October 2003. ICWS-Europe'03 was an extended event of the 2003 International Conference on Web Services (ICWS 2003) in Europe. In 2004 ICWS-Europe changed to the European Conference on Web Services (ECOWS), which was held in Erfurt, Germany.

SCF 2019 was held successfully during June 25–30, 2019 in San Diego, USA. Affected by COVID-19, SCF 2020 was held online successfully during September 18–20, 2020, and SCF 2021 was held virtually during December 10–14, 2021.

Celebrating its 20-year birthday, the 2022 Services Conference Federation (SCF 2022, www.icws.org) was a hybrid conference with a physical onsite in Honolulu, Hawaii, USA, satellite sessions in Shenzhen, Guangdong, China, and also online sessions for those who could not attend onsite. All virtual conference presentations were given via prerecorded videos in December 10–14, 2022 through the BigMarker Video Broadcasting Platform: https://www.bigmarker.com/series/services-conference-federati/series_summit.

Just like SCF 2022, SCF 2023 will most likely be a hybrid conference with physical onsite and virtual sessions online, it will be held in September 2023.

To present a new format and to improve the impact of the conference, we are also planning an Automatic Webinar which will be presented by experts in various fields. All the invited talks will be given via prerecorded videos and will be broadcast in a live-like format recursively by two session channels during the conference period. Each invited talk will be converted into an on-demand webinar right after the conference.

In the past 19 years, the ICWS community has expanded from Web engineering innovations to scientific research for the whole services industry. Service delivery platforms have been expanded to mobile platforms, the Internet of Things, cloud computing, and edge computing. The services ecosystem has been enabled gradually, with value added and intelligence embedded through enabling technologies such as Big Data, artificial intelligence, and cognitive computing. In the coming years, all transactions involving multiple parties will be transformed to blockchain.

Based on technology trends and best practices in the field, the Services Conference Federation (SCF) will continue to serve as a forum for all services-related conferences. SCF 2022 defined the future of the new ABCDE (AI, Blockchain, Cloud, Big Data & IOT). We are very proud to announce that SCF 2023's 10 colocated theme topic conferences will all center around "services", while each will focus on exploring different themes (Web-based services, cloud-based services, Big Data-based services, services innovation lifecycles, AI-driven ubiquitous services, blockchain-driven trust service ecosystems, Metaverse services and applications, and emerging service-oriented technologies).

The 10 colocated SCF 2023 conferences will be sponsored by the Services Society, the world-leading not-for-profit organization dedicated to serving more than 30,000 services computing researchers and practitioners worldwide. A bigger platform means bigger opportunities for all volunteers, authors, and participants. Meanwhile, Springer will provide sponsorship for Best Paper Awards. All 10 conference proceedings of SCF 2023 will be published by Springer, and to date the SCF proceedings have been indexed in the ISI Conference Proceedings Citation Index (included in the Web of Science), the Engineering Index EI (Compendex and Inspec databases), DBLP, Google Scholar, IO-Port, MathSciNet, Scopus, and ZbMath.

SCF 2023 will continue to leverage the invented Conference Blockchain Model (CBM) to innovate the organizing practices for all 10 conferences. Senior researchers in the field are welcome to submit proposals to serve as CBM ambassadors for individual conferences.

SCF 2023 Events

The 2023 edition of the Services Conference Federation (SCF) will include 10 service-oriented conferences: ICWS, CLOUD, SCC, BigData Congress, AIMS, METAVERSE, ICIOT, EDGE, ICCC and ICBC.

The 2023 International Conference on Web Services (ICWS 2023, http://icws.org/2023) will be the flagship theme-topic conference for Web-centric services, enabling technologies and applications.

The 2023 International Conference on Cloud Computing (CLOUD 2023, http://thecloudcomputing.org/2023) will be the flagship theme-topic conference for resource sharing, utility-like usage models, IaaS, PaaS, and SaaS.

The 2023 International Conference on Big Data (BigData 2023, http://bigdatacongress.org/2023) will be the theme-topic conference for data sourcing, data processing, data analysis, data-driven decision-making, and data-centric applications.

The 2023 International Conference on Services Computing (SCC 2023, http://thescc.org/2023) will be the flagship theme-topic conference for leveraging the latest computing technologies to design, develop, deploy, operate, manage, modernize, and redesign business services.

The 2023 International Conference on AI & Mobile Services (AIMS 2023, http://ai1000.org/2023) will be a theme-topic conference for artificial intelligence, neural networks, machine learning, training data sets, AI scenarios, AI delivery channels, and AI supporting infrastructures, as well as mobile Internet services. AIMS will bring AI to mobile devices and other channels.

The 2023 International Conference on Metaverse (Metaverse 2023, http://www.metaverse1000.org/2023) will focus on innovations of the services industry, including financial services, education services, transportation services, energy services, government services, manufacturing services, consulting services, and other industry services.

The 2023 International Conference on Cognitive Computing (ICCC 2023, http://thecognitivecomputing.org/2023) will focus on leveraging the latest computing technologies to simulate, model, implement, and realize cognitive sensing and brain operating systems.

The 2023 International Conference on Internet of Things (ICIOT 2023, http://iciot.org/2023) will focus on the science, technology, and applications of IOT device innovations as well as IOT services in various solution scenarios.

The 2023 International Conference on Edge Computing (EDGE 2023, http://theedgecomputing.org/2023) will be a theme-topic conference for leveraging the latest computing technologies to enable localized device connections, edge gateways, edge applications, edge-cloud interactions, edge-user experiences, and edge business models.

The 2023 International Conference on Blockchain (ICBC 2023, http://blockchain1000.org/2023) will concentrate on all aspects of blockchain, including digital currencies, distributed application development, industry-specific blockchains, public blockchains, community blockchains, private blockchains, blockchain-based services, and enabling technologies.

Contents

FRSM: A Novel Fault-Tolerant Approach for Redundant-Path-Enabled Service Migration in Mobile Edge Computing

Jiale Zhao[1], Mengxuan Dai[2], Yunni Xia[1(✉)], Yong Ma[2], Meibin He[3],
Kai Peng[4], Jianqi Li[5], Fan Li[6], and Xiaodong Fu[7]

[1] School of Computer, Chongqing University, Chongqing 400030, China
xiayunni@hotmail.com
[2] School of Computer and Information Engineering, Jiangxi Normal University,
Nanchang 330022, China
[3] Department of Big Data and AI of Jiangxi Telecom, Nanchang 330029, China
[4] Engineering College, Huaqiao University, Quanzhou 362021, China
[5] Global Energy Interconnection Research Institute Co. Ltd., Beijing 102209, China
[6] Key Laboratory of Fundamental Synthetic Vision Graphics and Image Science
for National Defense, Sichuan University, Chengdu 610065, China
[7] Data Science Research Center, Faculty of Science, Kunming University of Science
and Technology, Kunming 650031, China

Abstract. Mobile Edge Computing (MEC) provides users with low-latency, highly responsive services by deploying Edge Servers (ESs) near applications. MEC allows any edge-hosted application or service to be migrated between different edge resource providers without being locked into a single provider. Nevertheless, due to its complexity and dynamics, the real edge computing environment is prone to errors and failures, reducing the reliability of edge service migration. This paper proposes a novel fault-tolerant method for redundant path service migration. The method utilizes sliding-window-based model and identifies a set of service migration paths, enabling the evaluation of the time-varying failure rate of ESs. The method combines resubmission and replication mechanisms and decides the edge service migration scheme by selecting multiple redundant migration paths. We also conduct extensive simulations and show that our proposed method outperforms traditional solutions in several metrics.

Keywords: Mobile edge computing · Service migration ·
Fault-tolerant · Resubmission · Replication

This work is supported by Postgraduate Scientific Research and Innovation Foundation of Chongqing under Grant No. CYB22064; This work is supported by National Science Foundations under Grant Nos. 6217206 and 62162036. This work is extended from our previous publication of https://doi.org/10.3390/app12199987.

1   Introduction

Mobile edge computing has important research significance and practical value as an essential branch in real-time service computing [1–3]. When an edge node lacks functions or is overloaded and cannot provide services, MEC allows the tasks performed on the node to be migrated between different resource providers or edge nodes [4,5]. Nevertheless, the edge computing infrastructure is prone to errors due to the dynamic and decentralized nature of mobile edge computing [6,7].

To ensure reliable service migration, edge service providers must strengthen fault-tolerance as a countermeasure against failure [8]. Among the various fault-tolerant strategies, replication and resubmission are two basic fault-tolerant strategies that are widely used and have been proven to have high capabilities in MEC. Replication-based fault-tolerance refers to running multiple redundant copies of each service. It effectively prevents failures of components or individual resources from interrupting system-level task flow, thereby improving service execution efficiency. Resubmission-based fault-tolerance refers to re-executing failed tasks on the same or another processing unit. It can improve system resource utilization and prevent business interruption caused by task execution failure. Researchers have proposed several fault-tolerance schemes based on replication and resubmission [9–14].

This paper combines replication-based and resubmission-based fault-tolerant technologies, and propose a novel fault-tolerant approach for redundant-path-enabled service migration in MEC, called FRSM. First, using a sliding-window-based model, FRSM can evaluate the time-varying failure rate of ESs and obtain a set of optimal migration paths. Then, take the replication fault-tolerance as a whole, and adopt the resubmission fault-tolerance mechanism on each migration path to ensure the efficiency of edge service migration by using their respective advantages.

2   Related Work

In recent years, Quality of Service (QoS) guarantees and fault-tolerance have received extensive attention in edge service migration [15–24]. Intuitively, you can reduce transmission errors simply by reducing the amount of data that needs to be migrated. Therefore, Ha *et al.* [16] execute incremental coding, deduplication and data compression successively before service migration to reduce the amount of data transmission and improve the efficiency of service migration. For large-scale MEC environments, Zhao *et al.* [17] proposed an optimization method to find the best migration path to reduce data migration overhead and save costs. Qiao *et al.* [18] uses collaborative edge caching to obtain better computing results with lower computational complexity. Peng *et al.* [19] formulates task migration as an online multidimensional integer linear programming problem and proposed a decentralized response method that uses a dynamic learning mechanism to generate online migration decisions.

Long *et al.* [20] adopts the Primary-Backup (PB) mechanism to perform fault-tolerance on service migration, and uses the Deep Q-Network (DQN) to solve the problem. Xu *et al.* [21] adopts the Pareto optimal method to comprehensively consider multiple indicators, select multiple suitable migration paths for synchronous migration, and achieve the purpose of fault-tolerance. Still, the change of ESs failure rate was not considered. Jhawar *et al.* [22] proposed to ensure the QoS of the system through a fault-tolerant strategy provided by a third party. Plankensteiner *et al.* [23] proposed replication and resubmission of each service simultaneously in MEC and adjusting the replica size by using the effect of service resubmission, thus a trade-off between the two fault-tolerance strategies. Similarly, on the premise that the failure rate of ESs is fixed, Yao *et al.* [24] proposes a workflow fault-tolerant scheduling algorithm based on resource imbalance by combining two fault-tolerant strategies of replication and resubmission.

Notation	Definition
B	The set of base stations
N	The set of network routers
R	The set of tasks
M^{r_i}	The set of Migration paths for task r_i
MT_i	The Migration time of task r_i
b_i	The i-th base station in B
n_i	The i-th network router in N
r_i	The i-th task in R
$m_j^{r_i}$	The j-th Migration path in M^{r_i}
l_i^b	The coordinates of b_i
f_i^b	The signal coverage radius of b_i
e_i^b	The edge server of b_i
c_i^b	The residual computing power of e_i
sw_i^b	The task information performed on the e_i in the recent period
l_i^n	The coordinates of n_i
f_i^n	The failure rate of n_i
a_i^r	The arrival time of r_i
d_i^r	The amount of data transmitted in r_i
td_i^r	The maximum tolerable time of r_i
l_i^r	The coordinates of r_i
p_i^r	The amount of calculation of r_i
t_i^j	The execution time of task r_i on e_j
$t_i^{j'}$	The normalized data of t_i^j
y_i^j	The number of edge servers in $m_j^{r_i}$
bw_{xy}	The bandwidth between node x and node y
$d_i^{r'}$	The calculation result of d_i^r
β	The channel bandwidth of the base station
ρ_i	The signal transmission power of r_i
λ^2	The Gaussian noise power of the device

Fig. 1. Summary of notations

3 System Model and Problem Description

3.1 System Model

In the MEC environment proposed in this paper, the ESs are deployed in the Base Stations (BSs) near the user side. For ease of presentation, ESs and BSs in this paper can express the same meaning to some extent, although not strictly. The set $B = \{b_1, b_2, ..., b_m\}$ to denotes m BSs deployed within a certain range, each BS is represented by a triple (l_i^b, f_i^b, e_i^b). The set $N = \{n_1, n_2, ..., n_k\}$ to denotes k Network Routers (NRs) deployed within a certain range, each NR is represented by a two-tuple (l_i^n, f_i^n). The set $R = \{r_1, r_2, ..., r_n\}$ to denotes the services that Edge Users (ESs) need to migrate. In our proposed model, services and tasks represent the same thing. Each service is defined by a quintuple $(a_i^r, d_i^r, td_i^r, l_i^r, p_i^r)$. All symbols appearing in this paper are shown in Fig. 1.

As illustrated in Fig. 2, when EU moves along a specific trajectory, the feasible service migration paths are as follows: ES1-NR1-NR5-ES5, ES1-NR1-NR4-ES5, ES1-NR2-ES3-NR5-ES5, etc. In our model, the set $M^{r_i} = \{m_1^{r_i}, m_2^{r_i}, ..., m_s^{r_i}\}$ denotes s migration paths of task r_i, and each path $m_j^{r_i}$ includes multiple ESs and BSs. As mentioned above, the performance of ESs may vary in real scenarios due to various objective factors. If the failure rate of NR1 in Fig. 2 is much greater than that of ES3, the obvious choice of ES1-NR2-ES3-NR5-ES5 for service migration is sensible.

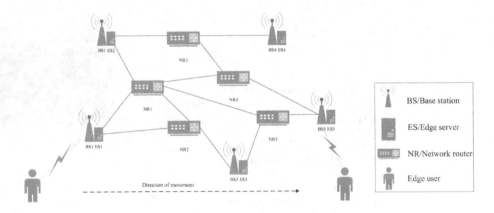

Fig. 2. Abstract network structure

The probability of failure of task r_i executed on edge server e_j^b is:

$$P_i^j(F \mid t_i^{j'}) = \frac{P_i^j(t_i^{j'} \mid F)P_i^j(F)}{P_i^j(t_i^{j'})} \tag{1}$$

$P_i^j(t_i^{j'} \mid F)$, $P_i^j(F)$, and $P_i^j(t_i^{j'})$ can be calculated according to sw_j^b. Where F denotes the migration failure, and $t_i^{j'}$ denotes the execution time t_i^j of task r_i on e_j^b to normalize data:

$$t_i^{j'} = \frac{t_i^j - t_{min}}{t_{max} - t_{min}} \tag{2}$$

where t_{max} and t_{min} respectively denotes the longest and shortest execution time of tasks in sw_j^b on e_j^b, and the execution time t_i^j is calculated as follows:

$$t_i^j = \frac{p_i^r}{y_i^k c_j^b} \tag{3}$$

where y_i^k denotes the number of ESs in $m_k^{r_i}$, p_i^r denotes the amount of computation required to complete r_i, and c_j^b denotes the remaining computing power in e_j^b.

MT_i^k of the total time of service migration of r_i on $m_k^{r_i}$ consists of task calculation time Z_i^k and data transmission time D_i^k:

$$MT_i^k = Z_i^k + D_i^k \tag{4}$$

Generally, the NRs provide forwarding services, not computing services, so all tasks are calculated in the ESs:

$$Z_i^k = \sum_{x=1}^{y_i^k} t_i^x + FZ_i^k \tag{5}$$

where FZ_i^k denotes the redundant calculation time, an optional item, and only needs to be calculated when ES fails.

D_i^k consists of the following four parts:

$$D_i^k = DU_i^k + DT_i^k + DD_i^k + FD_i^k \tag{6}$$

DU_i^k denotes the uplink transmission time of d_i^r from user equipment to ES:

$$DU_i^k = \frac{d_i^r}{\beta \log_2(1 + \frac{\rho_i}{\lambda^2})} \tag{7}$$

where β is the channel bandwidth of the BS, ρ_i is the signal transmission power of the mobile device, and λ^2 is the Gaussian noise power of edge device.

DT_i^k denotes the transit time of d_i^r between ESs and NRs:

$$DT_i^k = \sum_{(x,y) \in m_k^{r_i}} \frac{d_i^r}{bw_{xy}} \tag{8}$$

$(x,y) \in m_k^{r_i}$ denotes the record of r_i from node x to y, bw_{xy} denotes the bandwidth between x and y.

DD_i^k denotes the downlink transmission time for the data calculation result to be returned from the ES to user equipment:

$$DD_i^k = \frac{d_i^{r'}}{\beta \log_2(1 + \frac{\rho_i}{\lambda^2})} \tag{9}$$

where $d_i^{r'}$ indicates the calculation result of r_i.

FD_i^k indicates the redundant calculation time, an optional item, and only needs to be calculated when ES or NR fails.

3.2 Problem Description

This paper aims to solve the following problems: multiple ESs and NRs are deployed within a certain range, the service will pass through h nodes in the migration path p in this area, among which there are m ESs, how to choose appropriate migration path to reduce the failure rate of r_i migration to minimize execution time:

$$Min : \prod_{x=1}^{m} P_i^x(F \mid t_i^{x'}) \prod_{y=1}^{h-m} f_y^n \tag{10}$$

$$Min : MT_i^p \tag{11}$$

$$s.t : g(r_i) \in M \tag{12}$$

$$h(r_i) \in M \tag{13}$$

$$MT_i^p \leq td_i^r \tag{14}$$

$$0 \leq P_i^x(F \mid t_i^{x'}) < 1 \tag{15}$$

$$0 \leq f_y^n < 1 \tag{16}$$

Functions $g(r_i)$ and $h(r_i)$ indicates r_i arriving at source ES and migrating to target ES, respectively, M indicates the resource pool composed of m ESs, and MT_i^p indicates the migration time of the task.

4 FRSM: Fault-Tolerant Approach for Redundant-Path-Enabled Service Migration

4.1 Path Selection

Traditional MEC mainly studies the task offloading, data transmission, and resource scheduling of service migration [21]. Nevertheless, with the rapid growth of the complexity of mobile applications, simple data migration is difficult to meet the needs of EUs. Therefore, the case where services are migrated and computed at the same time are considered in this paper.

As shown in Fig. 3, we found the shortest path using Dijkstra algorithm, which is a simple and efficient . When explore the migration path of r_i, the weight of the ESs node in graph G is the failure rate of r_i when it is executed on e_j^b, i.e., $P_i^j(F \mid t_i^{j'})$. First, initialize the migration path set M^{r_i} and weight graph G (lines 1–2), then find the path m^{r_i} with the lowest failure rate according to the

---

Algorithm 1 Path Selection Algorithm

Input: Task r_i; source edge server B_s; target edge server B_t.
Output: T or F, where T indicates that the task migration succeeded, and F indicates that the task migration fail.
1: Initialize the set of migration paths $M^{r_i} \leftarrow \{\}$.
2: Abstracts the transmission link between B_s and B_t as a weighted graph G, the failure rate is the weight.
3: **while** True **do**
4:     apply Dijkstra algorithm to the weighted graph G to find the shortest path m^{r_i} from B_s to B_t
5:     **if** m^{r_i} not exists **then**
6:         break
7:     **else**
8:         $M^{r_i} \leftarrow M^{r_i} \cup \{m^{r_i}\}$
9:         delete path m^{r_i}
10:     **end if**
11: **end while**
12: **if** $M^{r_i} == \varnothing$ **then**
13:     return F
14: **else**
15:     compute the task migration time MT_i
16:     **if** $MT_i > td_i^r$ **then**
17:         return F
18:     **else**
19:         return T
20:     **end if**
21: **end if**

Fig. 3. Path Selection Algorithm

Dijkstra algorithm, add m^{r_i} to M^{r_i}, delete this link in the m^{r_i}, and cyclically find all paths (lines 3–9), and finally determine whether the service is successfully migrated (lines 10–21). The task migration time MT_i is the shortest migration time of task r_i in all feasible paths, which will be described in detail later.

To ensure the success rate of business migration, the FRSM algorithm searches for all feasible paths in G for migration, which is not applicable to all situations. If all migration paths are found in a dense network, the cost of migration will be immeasurable. Nevertheless, as long as the FRSM algorithm is slightly modified, it can be applied to a broader range of situations. For example, limiting the number of migration paths or the number of nodes in a migration path can well solve the problem of high migration costs.

4.2 Service Migration

In business migration, the FRSM algorithm first copies tasks into multiple copies, and then migrates them simultaneously on all feasible paths. There is no need to worry about the ESs recalculating multiple identical tasks during migration.

Algorithm 2 Service Migration Algorithm

Input: Task r_i; All feasible migration paths M^{r_i}.
Output: The task migration time MT_i.
1: Initialize the task migration time $MT_i = \infty$.
2: **for all** $m^{r_i} \in M^{r_i}$ **do**
3:     Initialize the task transfer time $D_i^{m^{r_i}} = 0$
4:     Initialize the task execution time $Z_i^{m^{r_i}} = 0$
5:     **for all** $n \in m^{r_i}$ **do**
6:         **if** n is the edge server **then**
7:             $D_i^{m^{r_i}} = D_i^{m^{r_i}} + D_i^n \leftarrow$ compute the task transfer time of r_i on n according to (6)
8:             $Z_i^{m^{r_i}} = Z_i^{m^{r_i}} + Z_i^n \leftarrow$ compute the task execution time of r_i on n according to (5)
9:             **if** n fail **then**
10:                 **if** n is source edge server **then**
11:                     $D_i^{m^{r_i}} = \infty$
12:                     break
13:                 **else**
14:                     add the information of task r_i to sw_n^b
15:                     roll back to the previous node
16:                 **end if**
17:             **else**
18:                 add the information of task r_i to sw_n^b
19:             **end if**
20:         **else**
21:             $D_i^{m^{r_i}} = D_i^{m^{r_i}} + D_i^n \leftarrow$ compute the task transfer time of r_i on n according to (6)
22:             **if** n fail **then**
23:                 roll back to the previous node
24:             **end if**
25:         **end if**
26:     **end for**
27:     **if** $D_i^{m^{r_i}} + Z_i^{m^{r_i}} < MT_i$ **then**
28:         $MT_i = D_i^{m^{r_i}} + Z_i^{m^{r_i}}$
29:     **end if**
30: **end for**
31: return MT_i

Fig. 4. Service Migration Algorithm

First of all, when searching for the migration path in Fig. 3, all duplicate data links have been deleted (line 9), so there will not be the same data links in the migration path. Second, assume that two replicated tasks arrive at the same ES simultaneously (via different links, although the probability of this happening is very low). In this case, ES will only compute any of these tasks and duplicate the result since both tasks will be sent to the following different node. Because the two tasks are the same, the calculation results are also the same, and the cost of copying the calculation results is small and does not affect the final result.

During the task migration process, if the ESs fails, the task will be rolled back to the previous node and then resent to the ES for processing. When the task on a path in M^{r_i} reaches the target ES successfully, a termination instruction will be sent to terminate the service migration on other paths to save costs. This is easy to achieve because each task includes all migration paths. The transmission time of the termination instruction is negligible, so it can quickly terminate task migrations on other paths.

To facilitate understanding, Fig. 4 describes the service migration strategy of the FRSM algorithm in a circular form. The migration time (lines 1–26) of each path m^{r_i} in the path set M^{r_i} of task r_i was calculated respectively, and the path with the shortest migration time was the actual migration path of task r_i (lines 27–31). It should be noted that, as shown in lines 9–19 and 22–23, if a task fails to be rolled back, its final migration time will need to be added with the rollback calculation time, which is reflected in the form of redundant calculation time in this model.

5   Performance Evaluation

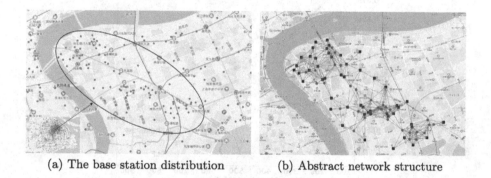

(a) The base station distribution   (b) Abstract network structure

Fig. 5. Pudong Central Business District

The simulation experiment is based on the real edge environment data sets Telecom [25–27] and Taxi [28]. As illustrated in Fig. 5, in the Telecom data set, 80 BSs in Pudong Central Business District are selected for simulation experiments, and 30 base stations are randomly selected as NRs.

We consider Average Completion Time (ACT), Task Completion Rate (TCR) and Average Failure Count (AFC) as the metrics. We use PLP [21], FRSM/F[1] and Greedy[2] as the peers. In the "AFC" benchmark, FRSM/AP and

---

[1] It is a simplified version of the FRSM algorithm, where the failure rate of ESs is constant.

[2] It is a traditional greedy algorithm, which first finds the current closest path and performs service migration based on the resubmission strategy.

FRSM/F/AP indicate the average number of migration failures in all migration paths, and FRSM/OP and FRSM/F/OP indicate the average number of migration failures in successful migration paths.

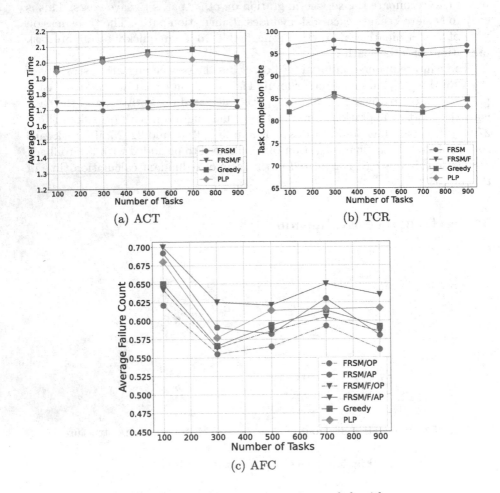

(a) ACT

(b) TCR

(c) AFC

Fig. 6. Three performance comparisons of algorithms

As illustrated in Fig. 6, compared with the FRSM/F algorithm, the FRSM algorithm improves the performance of ACT, TCR, and AFC by 1.93%, 2.18%, and 2.97%, respectively. Compared with the PLP algorithm, the FRSM algorithm has improved by 14.66%, 13.9%, and 7.22% in the three performance indicators, respectively. Compared with Greedy, the FRSM algorithm has improved by 15.89%, 14.32%, and 4.18% in the three performance indicators, respectively.

6   Conclusion

This paper proposes a fault-tolerant service migration method (FRSM) for service migration in the MEC environment. To verify the performance of FRSM, we conduct simulation experiments based on two real MEC datasets. The experimental results show that compared with the traditional service migration method, FRSM can significantly improve the task completion rate and the average task completion time. In future work, we plan to use reinforcement learning with strong robustness and good generalization to solve problems e.g., load balancing scheduling and ES performance prediction in MEC to further reduce transmission costs improve system QoS.

References

1. Weisong, S., Xingzhou, Z., Yifan, W., Qingyang, Z.: Edge computing: state-of-the-art and future directions. J. Comput. Res. Dev. **56**(1), 69 (2019)
2. Hu, Y.C., Patel, M., Sabella, D., Sprecher, N., Young, V.: Mobile edge computing-a key technology towards 5g. ETSI white pap. **11**(11), 1–16 (2015)
3. Deng, S., et al.: Toward mobile service computing: opportunities and challenges. IEEE Cloud Comput. **3**(4), 32–41 (2016)
4. Wang, S., Urgaonkar, R., He, T., Chan, K., Zafer, M., Leung, K.K.: Dynamic service placement for mobile micro-clouds with predicted future costs. IEEE Trans. Parallel Distrib. Syst. **28**(4), 1002–1016 (2016)
5. Satyanarayanan, M., Bahl, P., Caceres, R., Davies, N.: The case for VM-based cloudlets in mobile computing. IEEE Pervasive Comput. **8**(4), 14–23 (2009)
6. Pezoa, J.E., Dhakal, S., Hayat, M.M.: Maximizing service reliability in distributed computing systems with random node failures: theory and implementation. IEEE Trans. Parallel Distrib. Syst. **21**(10), 1531–1544 (2010)
7. Plankensteiner, K., Prodan, R.: Meeting soft deadlines in scientific workflows using resubmission impact. IEEE Trans. Parallel Distrib. Syst. **23**(5), 890–901 (2011)
8. Poola, D., Ramamohanarao, K., Buyya, R.: Enhancing reliability of workflow execution using task replication and spot instances. ACM Trans. Autonom. Adapt. Syst. (TAAS) **10**(4), 1–21 (2016)
9. Chen, W., Lee, Y.C., Fekete, A., Zomaya, A.Y.: Adaptive multiple-workflow scheduling with task rearrangement. J. Supercomput. **71**(4), 1297–1317 (2015). https://doi.org/10.1007/s11227-014-1361-0
10. Olteanu, A., Pop, F., Dobre, C., Cristea, V.: A dynamic rescheduling algorithm for resource management in large scale dependable distributed systems. Comput. Math. Appl. **63**(9), 1409–1423 (2012)
11. Cao, Y., Ro, C., Yin, J.: Scheduling Analysis of failure-aware VM in cloud system. Int. J. Control Autom. **7**(1), 243–250 (2014)
12. Jing, W., Liu, Y.: Multiple DAGs reliability model and fault-tolerant scheduling algorithm in cloud computing system. Comput. Model. New Technol. **18**(8), 22–30 (2014)
13. Jayadivya, S.K., Nirmala, J.S., Bhanu, M.S.S.: Fault tolerant workflow scheduling based on replication and resubmission of tasks in cloud computing. Int. J. Comput. Sci. Eng. **4**(6), 996 (2012)

14. Patra, P.K., Singh, H., Singh, R., Das, S., Dey, N., Victoria, A.D.C.: Replication and resubmission based adaptive decision for fault tolerance in real time cloud computing: a new approach. Int. J. Serv. Sci. Manage. Eng. Technol. (IJSSMET) **7**(2), 46–60 (2016)
15. Plachy, J., Becvar, Z., Mach, P.: Path selection enabling user mobility and efficient distribution of data for computation at the edge of mobile network. Comput. Netw. **108**, 357–370 (2016)
16. Ha, K., et al.: Adaptive VM handoff across cloudlets. Technical Report CMU-CS-15-113 (2015)
17. Zhao, F., Zeng, X.: Optimization of user and operator cost for large-scale transit network. J. Transp. Eng. **133**(4), 240–251 (2007)
18. Qiao, G., Leng, S., Maharjan, S., Zhang, Y., Ansari, N.: Deep reinforcement learning for cooperative content caching in vehicular edge computing and networks. IEEE Internet Things J. **7**(1), 247–257 (2019)
19. Peng, Q., Xia, Y., Wang, Y., Wu, C., Luo, X., Lee, J.: A decentralized reactive approach to online task offloading in mobile edge computing environments. In: Kafeza, E., Benatallah, B., Martinelli, F., Hacid, H., Bouguettaya, A., Motahari, H. (eds.) ICSOC 2020. LNCS, vol. 12571, pp. 232–247. Springer, Cham (2020). https://doi.org/10.1007/978-3-030-65310-1_18
20. Long, T., Chen, P., Xia, Y., Jiang, N., Wang, X., Long, M.: A novel fault-tolerant approach to web service composition upon the edge computing environment. In: Xu, C., Xia, Y., Zhang, Y., Zhang, L.J. (eds.) Web Services – ICWS 2021. ICWS 2021. Lecture Notes in Computer Science, vol. 12994, pp. 15–31. Springer, Cham (2021). https://doi.org/10.1007/978-3-030-96140-4_2
21. Xu, J., Ma, X., Zhou, A., Duan, Q., Wang, S.: Path selection for seamless service migration in vehicular edge computing. IEEE Internet Things J. **7**(9), 9040–9049 (2020)
22. Jhawar, R., Piuri, V., Santambrogio, M.: Fault tolerance management in cloud computing: a system-level perspective. IEEE Syst. J. **7**(2), 288–297 (2012)
23. Plankensteiner, K., Prodan, R.: Meeting soft deadlines in scientific workflows using resubmission impact. IEEE Trans. Parallel Distrib. Syst. **23**(5), 890–901 (2011)
24. Yao, G., Ding, Y., Hao, K.: Using imbalance characteristic for fault-tolerant workflow scheduling in cloud systems. IEEE Trans. Parallel Distrib. Syst. **28**(12), 3671–3683 (2017)
25. Li, Y., Zhou, A., Ma, X., Wang, S.: Profit-aware edge server placement. IEEE Internet Things J. **9**(1), 55–67 (2021)
26. Guo, Y., Wang, S., Zhou, A., Xu, J., Yuan, J., Hsu, C.H.: User allocation-aware edge cloud placement in mobile edge computing. Softw. Pract. Experience **50**(5), 489–502 (2020)
27. Wang, S., Guo, Y., Zhang, N., Yang, P., Zhou, A., Shen, X.: Delay-aware microservice coordination in mobile edge computing: a reinforcement learning approach. IEEE Trans. Mob. Comput. **20**(3), 939–951 (2019)
28. Liu, S., Liu, Y., Ni, L.M., Fan, J., Li, M.: Towards mobility-based clustering. In: Proceedings of the 16th ACM SIGKDD international conference on Knowledge discovery and data mining, pp. 919–928 (2010)

A Novel Outlier-Tolerable and Predictive Approach to Web Service Composition

Xiaoning Sun[1], Peng Chen[2(✉)], Mengxuan Dai[3], Yunni Xia[4(✉)],
Wanbo Zheng[5], Jianqi Li[6], Hong Xie[4], Xiaodong Fu[5], Kai Peng[7],
Xianhua Niu[2], and Juan Chen[2]

[1] School of Computer and Information Science, Chongqing Normal University,
Chongqing 401331, China
[2] School of Computer and Software Engineering, Xihua University,
Chengdu 610039, China
chenpeng@mail.xhu.edu.cn
[3] School of Computer and Information Engineering, Jiangxi Normal University,
Nanchang 330022, China
[4] College of Computer Science, Chongqing University, Chongqing 400030, China
xiayunni@hotmail.com
[5] Data Science Research Center, Faculty of Science, Kunming University of Science
and Technology, Kunming 650031, China
[6] Global Energy Interconnection Research Institute Co. Ltd., Beijing 102209, China
[7] Engineering college, Huaqiao University, Quanzhou 362021, China

Abstract. The Quality-of-Service (QoS) aspects of Web service has
gained popularity in the field of service computing. QoS-oriented Web
service composition is a distributed model to construct new web service on top of existing primitive or other composite web services with
QoS guarantees. A major challenge in this field is that the QoS data of
candidate services are with run-time fluctuations and thus difficult to
predict. Traditional approaches in this direction tended to address the
challenge by statistics, prediction and neural network-based models. A
major limitation of these methods lies in that they ignore outliers data
in the historical QoS data, in terms of inconsistencies, errors, shifts, corruptions, etc. In this work, instead, we consider outliers in QoS series to
be non-neglectable, and propose an outlier-tolerable and predictive approach to service composition through leveraging a joint estimation-based
outlier detection method and a niched genetic algorithm. To validate the
effectiveness of our proposed method, we conduct extensive case studies
based on different outlier conditions, and the experimental results show
that our method is superior to existing ones.

Keywords: QoS · Service composition · Outliers · Niched genetic
algorithm

This work is supported by National Science Foundations with No. 62172062 and No.
62162036, and Chongqing Normal University Foundation with No. 22XLB016. Yunni
Xia is the first corresponding author (email: xiayunni@hotmail.com). Peng Chen is the
second corresponding author (email: chenpeng@mail.xhu.edu.cn).

Y. Zhang and L.-J. Zhang (Eds.): ICWS 2022, LNCS 13736, pp. 13–29, 2022.
https://doi.org/10.1007/978-3-031-23579-5_2

1   Introduction

With the development of cloud computing and big data mining technology, more and more Web services emerge on the Internet. In the face of the complexity of users' requests, it is increasingly challenging to select the candidate services that implement the functional requirements among the massive Web services and to assemble the composite services that meet the Quality-of-Service (QoS) constraints [1]. Simultaneously, increasing attention has been paid to the QoS aspects of service composition, which leverages historical QoS data for generating QoS-guaranteed service composition schedules. Due to the rapidly increasing pool of services providing the same or similar functionality, but differing in QoS, it is more challenging to select a service combination with optimal QoS performance, while satisfying user-oriented QoS requirements and considering the uncertainties in the collected data. The varying degrees of preference for different QoS properties signify the requested requirements. Computation of QoS attributes and their requested preferences is quintessential in ensuring a successful service composition. QoS criteria for SOA (Service-Oriented Architecture) systems include reliability, availability, latency, etc.

QoS data of candidate services are usually expressed through a series of measured quantitative records, i.e., time series. A time series dataset is a type of data that is collected over time and indexed in chronological order [2]. The purpose of time series data mining is to extract all the meaningful knowledge from the data, and then play a guiding role in the subsequent application. However, QoS series data is frequently corrupted by various kinds of interferences in the process of data collection, resulting in inconsistent and illogical observations with the surrounding values, i.e., outliers. Such sudden abnormal points in time series data will change the data trends temporarily or permanently. It is obvious that the inevitable outliers in the time series significantly affect the selection of prediction models, the estimation of parameters, the accuracy of prediction, and ultimately the user-perceived QoS of composite services. Therefore, outliers in service QoS data are supposed to be well taken into account and utilized in the process of service composition.

In the service-oriented environment, the Web services provided by service providers or the third party agents may fail partially or fully in delivering the promised QoS at runtime, which obviously span diverse computing platforms and organizations [3]. So some predictive methods are proposed to predict the runtime QoS values [4–6]. In the field of service composition, the traditional prediction methods usually consider that the historical QoS data of services are 100 percent trustworthy and accurate [1,4,7]. In fact, the complex network environment, the use of heterogeneous set of technologies and participants, the deployment of many unsafe nodes and illegal operations generally result in the QoS outliers in reality, in terms of inconsistencies, errors, shifts, corruptions, etc., in time series data, and then influence the preciseness of services scheduling. In this work, we consider that QoS data of services are expressed through time series with outliers and develop predictive and outlier-tolerable service composition method based on an improved niche genetic algorithm for generating service composition schedules. To illustrate the effectiveness of our approach, a number of case studies are performed based on a service composition template and a real QoS dataset. The experimental results show that the performance of our method clearly beats existing solution when QoS data are with varying conditions of outliers.

2   Related Work

The QoS-aware issue has always been a hotpot in the field of service computing. Similarly, it is indispensable to conduct QoS prediction in the process of service composition. Sun et al. [4] adopt ARIMA model to predict time series data and then input the prediction results to the service composition. Wang et al. [7] consider that the network delays in candidate services affect the performance of composite services, so they propose a geolocation-based service selection algorithm and a NQoS prediction method for service composition. Their experiments show the improvement in prediction accuracy and reduction in runtime overheads. Li et al. [8] design a new method, QSPC, to predict the QoS by leveraging the context data (mapping raw data to low-dimensional manifold space) and the request temporal information (proposing a sequence-to-sequence layer to capture the implicit factors of QoS). Li et al. [9] consider the sparsity and imbalance of QoS data and propose probability distribution detection-based hybrid ensemble QoS prediction model. In this paper, the prediction results generated by an enhanced collaborative filtering and the probability confidence weights calculated by other basic prediction models are combined to improve the prediction accuracy and scalability. In addition, some other works also adopt probability distribution to estimate QoS values. For example, Zheng et al. [10] estimate the QoS values of composite services based on QoS probability distribution of component services in the execution path. Similarly, Wang et al. [11] assume that the cost-performance index of services and the cost function of tasks follow a given probabilistic distribution. Hwang et al. [12,13] consider QoS of services to obey discrete probabilistic distribution, which can be estimated based on observed QoS records. Since the real-world QoS data exhibits two natural features of the low-rank structure and the clustered representation, Yu et al. [14] amalgamate them into one unified function by exploiting trace norm regularized matrix factorization to predict QoS values. In order to avoid threatening the information security in the process of QoS data collection, Zhu et al. [15] develop a novel algorithm that could make predictions based on location information (continent, longitude and latitude) while protecting user's privacy. In addition, some works are devoted to QoS prediction inspired by the deep learning. For instance, Wu et al. [16] propose a deep neural model (DNM) armed with the embedding layer, the interaction layer and the perception layer to realize multiple attributes QoS prediction with contexts. Xu et al. [17] employ the echo state network(ESN) in conjunction with a highly adaptive elastic net algorithm to predict multivariate time series.

The above works focus on the fluctuation and sparsity of QoS data, but they ignore the fact that outliers exist in time series data. The time series data is frequently corrupted by a wide variety of interferences in the process of data collection, resulting in inconsistent observations that deviate so much from other observations and further changing the trend and pattern of original data. And the outlier values explicitly influence the model selection, parameter estimation, and hence prediction effectiveness. Therefore, it necessitates detecting outliers before leveraging historical QoS data for service composition.

In recent years, outlier detection of time series data attracts considerable research attentions [18–23] in the field of data mining. Yu *et al.* [24] built an outlier detection model based on sliding window prediction and apply it in hydrological time series data. The sliding window splits the time data into sub-sequences. And the predictive results are generated by the autoregressive prediction model which is built from its nearest-neighbor-window. According to different size of the nearest-neighbor-window and confidence coefficient, the outliers can be dynamically identified as the observed values that fall outside the given prediction confidence interval (PCI). Liu *et al.* [25] propose an outlier detection algorithm based on SOM (Self-Organizing Maps) neural network. The detection strategy finds the isolated clusters in the results of the clustering algorithm by leveraging trained SOM neural network. In work [26], an unsupervised and nonparametric approach, UN-AVOIDS, is introduced for both visualization and detection of outliers. This approach transforms data to the neighborhood cumulative density function (NCDF) space, where both the detection algorithm and the analyst can see the same information, and hence, both the visualization and the auto-detection can work simultaneously and cooperatively. A classic outlier detection algorithm based on ARIMA model is proposed in work [27]. It's a kind of joint estimation method of model parameters and outlier effects in time series, which is able to modify the model parameters and detect outliers at the same time. YAHOO implemented an automatic outlier detection package, tsoutlier, following the procedure described in [27]. And this R language package has been constantly updating its version in recent years.

Although there are many researches on QoS prediction algorithm and time series outlier detection algorithm, yet to the best of our knowledge, there is no effort on QoS outlier detection in the process of service combination at present. As the outliers in QoS data bring considerable impact on selection of prediction models, the estimation of parameters, the accuracy of prediction, and ultimately the the performance of service composition, this work proposes a predictive algorithm for service composition based on outlier detection.

3   Predictive Service Composition Model Based on Outlier Detection

It is well known that Autoregressive Integrated Moving Average (ARIMA) model is a mature method for predicting time series data. Given a time series $\{X_t\}$, its

ARIMA model can be expressed as:

$$\phi(B)\alpha(B)X_t = \theta(B)\varepsilon_t, t = 1, ..., n \tag{1}$$

where $\phi(B)$ is the autoregression polynomial of B, $\theta(B)$ the moving average polynomial of B, and $\alpha(B)$ is the difference factor that makes the data stationary. Stated differently,

$$X_t = \frac{\theta(B)}{\phi(B)\alpha(B)}\varepsilon_t, t = 1, ..., n \tag{2}$$

But unsystematic outliers can not be captured by standard time series models. Therefore, assuming that there are m outliers in the time series at time $t_1, t_2, ..., t_m$, the model can be modified to:

$$X_t^* = \sum_{j=1}^{m} \omega_j L_j(B) I_t(t_j) + X_t = \sum_{j=1}^{m} \omega_j L_j(B) I_t(t_j) + \frac{\theta(B)}{\phi(B)\alpha(B)}\varepsilon_t \tag{3}$$

where $I_t(t_j)$ indicates whether there is an outlier at time $t = t_j$ (i.e., if j^{th} value is outlier when $t = t_j$, $I_t(t_j) = 1$; otherwise, $I_t(t_j) = 0$); $L_j(B)$ the type of the jth outlier; ω_j the influence weight of the jth outlier.

There may be multiple types of outliers in time series. According to the frequency of outliers, they can be divided into two categories: point outliers that behave abnormal at a specific moment when compared with other values in the time series and subsequence outliers that are the continuous points in time whose joint behavior is unusual. According to the influence of outliers on time series, they can be divided into Innovational Outlier (IO), Additive Outlier (AO), Temporary Change Outlier (TC) and Level Shift Outlier (LS). This approach is to classify an outlier impact into four types by imposing the special structure formulated as the following formula (4). The more detailed discussion on the outlier types can be found in [27].

$$\begin{aligned} IO &: L(B) = \frac{\theta(B)}{\alpha(B)\phi(B)} \\ AO &: L(B) = 1 \\ TC &: L(B) = \frac{1}{1 - \delta B} \\ LS &: L(B) = \frac{1}{1 - B} \end{aligned} \tag{4}$$

Define polynomial $\pi(B)$ as:

$$\pi(B) = \frac{\phi(B)\alpha(B)}{\theta(B)} = 1 - \pi_1 B - \pi_2 B - \text{,,,,} \tag{5}$$

Affected by outliers, the estimated residual $\hat{e}_t$ is:

$$\hat{e}_t = \pi(B)X_t^* \tag{6}$$

So,

$$\hat{e}_t = \pi(B)X_t^* = \sum_{j=1}^{m} \omega_j \pi(B)L_j(B)I_t(t_j) + \varepsilon_t \tag{7}$$

In this work, we adopt a joint estimation method [27] based on the above theory to perform outlier detection and ARIMA model fitting. The specific steps of the algorithm are summarized as follows:

1. Initializing model parameters.The parameters of the preliminary model are obtained by maximum likelihood estimation, i.e., given an ARIMA model fitted with original data;
2. Detecting outliers. According to the regression equation in formula (7), the corresponding t-statistics of residuals are calculated to detect and locate outliers by checking the significance of all types of outliers at all possible time points.
3. Estimating model parameters and removing outliers effects. The ARIMA model is re-fitted according to the potential outliers detected in step 2 and formula (3). Similarly, the potential outliers are reassessed and those non-significant outliers are deleted. The time series is adjusted to a new one by removing the outlier effects.
4. Iterating step 2 and step 3 if the relative change of the residual standard error from the previous estimate is less than the predetermined threshold value.

In a nutshell, we detect the locations of outliers, assess the outlier effects, and revise the parameters of the prediction model according to the adjusted time series in the iterative process. This outlier-tolerable prediction algorithm can eliminate the influence of outliers and get more accurate prediction results to guide the following service composition.

4 Service Composition Based on Niched Genetic Algorithm

4.1 Problem Description

As mentioned earlier, a complex user request is decomposed into n abstract tasks which are arranged in the form of service composition template to describe the internal logical structure. Thus a service composition template S with n abstract tasks can be denoted as $S = \{s_1, s_2, ..., s_n\}$. Each abstract task s_i in the template can be implemented by $m(i)$ competing candidate services with the identical function, represented as $\Omega(s_i) = \{s_{i,1}, s_{i,2}, ..., s_{i,m(i)}\}$. To describe QoS attributes of services, we define an r-dimensional array $Q(s_{i,j}) = < q^1(s_{i,j}), q^2(s_{i,j}), ..., q^r(s_{i,j}) >$, for each candidate service, where $s_{i,j}$ is the jth candidate for abstract task s_i, r the rth attribute in QoS set.

The global QoS constraints of composite services can be specified by users according to their preferences, denoted as $C = \{C^1, C^2, ..., C^r\}$. Specifically, given a composite service μ, its overall r^{th} dimension QoS should satisfy the constraint condition $q^r(\mu) \geq C^r$ if the rth attribute belongs to the category of positive QoS (namely $C^r \in Q^+$). Similarly, there is $q^r(\mu) \leq C^r$ if $C^r \in Q^-$. As the satisfaction of multiple constrains may be mutually contradictory, we use the utility function [28] formulated as (8),which transforms multi-objective optimization into single-objective optimization by applying preference weight w^r for different attributes r.

$$\max U(\mu)$$

$$= \sum_{r \in Q^+} \frac{q^r(\mu) - C^r}{C^r} \times w^r + \sum_{r \in Q^-} \frac{C^r - q^r(\mu)}{C^r} \times w^r$$

(8)

$$s.t. \ q^r(\mu) \geq C^r, \forall r \in Q^+$$
$$q^r(\mu) \leq C^r, \forall r \in Q^-$$

4.2   Niched Genetic Algorithm for Service Composition

As aforementioned, each task has many candidate services that can fulfill its functional requirements and various QoS attributes are mutually constrained. It is challenging to identify the optimal service composition instance under the condition of satisfying QoS constraints. Since this process is reducible to the knapsack problem, so this is a NP-complete problem. Genetic algorithm (GA) is recognized as a common and effective method to solve scheduling problems [28–32]. Since the limit of premature convergence in GA, the niched GA is proposed to avoid falling into local optimal solution.

In order to increase the diversity of the population in the process of evolution, a niched algorithm combining sharing mechanism and isolation mechanism is designed:

Sharing Mechanism. The individuals fitness is adjusted by sharing function to keep a certain distance between individuals and limit the large increase of certain individuals, so as to achieve the diversity of individuals in the population.

Isolation Mechanism. The isolation mechanism is implemented among populations for competition. According to the law of survival of the fittest, the higher the average fitness of each population, the larger the population size, and vice versa.

Populations Fusion. The optimal genome of the species is obtained through the populations fusion. The optimal individuals in a population that have evolved to a certain generation can achieve cross-population mating and reproduction.

Figure 1 shows the process of the improved niche genetic algorithm. The details of the process is presented as follows:

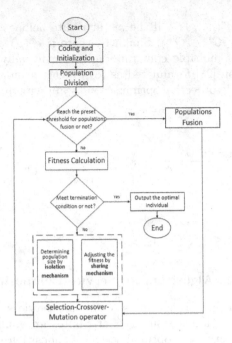

Fig. 1. The flow of niched genetic algorithm.

1. Coding

   Service composition is the process of finding the optimal composite service that can meet users' needs among multiple candidate services for each sub-task. For the purpose of transformation into the GA solution space, a possible composite service is regarded as a genome containing n genes, which is denoted as an array with n entries. And each entry in the array stands for the candidate service to fulfill the corresponding task. The initial Z individuals in species are randomly encoded, that is, candidate services performing task S_i are selected from their candidate service set $\{s_{i,1}, s_{i,2}, ..., s_{i,m(i)}\}$ at random.

2. Preliminary setting of populations

   The initial Z individuals are equally divided into K populations, each with Z/K genomes.

3. Calculating the fitness

   As mentioned above, the goal of service composition is to determine a service composition scheme that can maximize the utility value on the premise of satisfying various QoS constraints. Thus the fitness function is formulated as the combination of the utility value U and a penalty function P, defined in

(9).

$$F = U - w^P \times g \times P$$

$$P = \sum_{r \in Q} p^r$$

$$p^r = \begin{cases} \dfrac{C^r - q^r}{C^r}, & if \ \forall r \in Q^+ \ and \ q^r < C^r \\ \dfrac{q^r - C^r}{C^r}, & if \ \forall r \in Q^- \ and \ q^r > C^r \\ 0, & else \end{cases} \qquad (9)$$

The w^P is the penalty weight and g is the gth generation in the evolve. The fitness of all individuals in each population are calculated according to the above formula. For those individuals violating the constraints, their fitness decrease with the increase of generation g, so the individuals which meet the constraints and have high utility values tend to be selected.

4. Determining the population size by isolation mechanism

There is also competition among different populations for limited resources, so the population with higher overall fitness obtains better chance of thriving. Here, we use the following formulation to determine the offspring size of each population:

$$q_k^{g+1} = Z \times \overline{F_k^g} / \sum_{i=1}^{K} \overline{F_i^g} \qquad (10)$$

where Z is the overall size of all populations, K the number of population, $\overline{F_k^g}$ the average fitness of the kth population in the gth generation, and q_k^{g+1} the population size of the kth population in the next generation.

5. Adjusting the fitness by sharing mechanism

The fitness of individuals is adjusted by sharing function $f_s(d_{x,y})$, which describes the similarity between individuals x and y. And Hamming distance $d_{x,y}$ indicates the coding difference between two individuals, formulated as follows:

$$d_{x,y} = \sum_{i=1}^{n} (a_{xi} \bigoplus a_{yi}), x \in [1, z], y \in [1, z] \qquad (11)$$

where a_{xi} and a_{yi} represent the genes at position i in the genetic coding of individuals x and y, z is the number of individuals in a population, XOR operation obtains the coding difference between two individuals. So the sharing function is:

$$f_s(d_{x,y}) = \begin{cases} 1 - \dfrac{d_{x,y}}{\gamma}, & d_{x,y} < \gamma \\ 0, & d_{x,y} \geq \gamma \end{cases} \qquad (12)$$

where γ indicates niche radius and threshold of similarity between individuals. In the range of niche radius, the higher the similarity is, the greater the sharing function value. Individuals fitness values are adjusted according to the sharing function:

$$F'_x = F_x / \sum_{y=1}^{z} f_x(d_{x,y}) \tag{13}$$

The F_x is the original fitness of individual x, F'_x adjusted sharing fitness. The sharing fitness values of individuals with high similarity to others in the population decrease, thus ensuring the survival of individuals to maintain a certain distance, in other words, enabling individuals to disperse in the whole search space.

6. Selection-Crossover-Mutation operator

Each population is selected - crossed - mutated independently to generate offsprings. In the process of selection, the individual with the highest shared fitness is firstly retained, and the rest are generated by roulette procedure. Note that the selection operator is conducted based on the shared fitness obtained by the sharing mechanism and the population size obtained by the isolation mechanism. The crossover operator uses a Position-based-Crossover (PBX) scheme [33] to achieve multi-point crossover. The mutation operator adopts modulo-based method to ensure that the individuals after mutation still meet the coding rules [28].

7. Populations fusion

When generation g reaches a preset threshold G, individuals own the ability to reproduce across populations(i.e., across-populations fusion), and the top Z/K individuals of all populations are selected to form a new population to continue the selection-cross-mutation operator.

5   Experiments

5.1   Experimental Settings

To evaluate the effectiveness of our proposed algorithm, a series of simulated experiments are conducted through software R and MATLAB. The outlier-tolerable and predictive service composition is carried out based on Pegasus project's classic scientific template, CyberShake (Fig. 2), and the well-acknowledged QoS dataset [34] ,which records the real-world time series of response time and throughput.

In our experiments, each task was randomly assigned six candidate services from the dataset. The preference weight (w^r) of response time and throughput are both set to 0.5, and the penalty weight (w^P) in the GA is set to 0.1. The response time threshold (C^{rt}) is set as 3 s, and the throughput threshold (C^{th}) is set to 0.4 kbps.

In order to carry out the simulation experiment of outlier detection, we artificially inject some abnormal data at randomly selected positions in the original time series data. Specifically, we set a sliding window of size 5, which contains

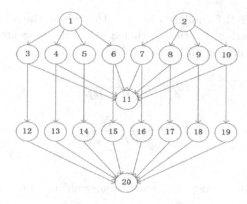

Fig. 2. The CyberShake template for service composition.

the data at the selected position b and the corresponding data at the contiguous positions from $b-2$ to $b+2$. And the mean value of the window data is taken for magnification to replace the original data at position b. In order to validate the effectiveness of our algorithm, we take the amplified values as 2 times, 4 times and 6 times respectively, so that we have three levels of outliers: low, medium and high. The number of outliers is also set to 5, 10 and 15 respectively. To examine the impact of the above two sets parameters on the result of outliers detection, we consider two groups of control experiments: when the outliers are generated by 4 times magnification, we test the influence of 5, 10 and 15 outliers respectively; when the outlier count is 10, the influence of three outlier levels are tested.

Based on preliminary tuning tests, the details of the genetic algorithm are set as follows: crossover probability is 0.7, mutation probability is 0.3. The species is divided into 10 populations and each one consists of 100 genomes. The niche radius is set as 15, and the threshold value G for across-populations fusion is set to 200. The termination condition of GA is the evolutionary process is iterated 300 times or there is no improvement on the optimal solution of continuous 100 generations. In order to eliminate the stochastic nature of GA, each experiment is performed 50 times and its average value is finally taken.

5.2 Experimental Evaluation

Evaluation of Outlier Detection

In this section, we validate the effectiveness and accuracy of outlier detection based on the two sets of parameters mentioned above. There are four possible outcomes of one detection run: True Positive (TP), False Negative (FN), False Positive (FP), and True Negative (TN). To be specific, TP represents the data points that are actual outliers and identified as outliers; FN represents the points that are actual outliers but identified as normal value; FP refers to the normal points which are incorrectly detected as outliers; TN refers to the normal points which are detected as normal. In addition, we also compute the sensitivity TPR and the specificity TNR formulated as (14)(15), where the TPR represents the probability of discovering a actual outlier and TNR represents the probability of correct detections among all normal values.

$$TPR = \frac{TP}{TP + FN} \tag{14}$$

$$TNR = \frac{TN}{FP + TN} \tag{15}$$

Table 1. Outlier detection results under different outlier levels

Outlier Levels	TP	TN	FP	FN	TPR	TNR
low	6	65	5	4	0.6	0.93
medium	8	69	1	2	0.8	0.99
high	9	70	0	1	0.9	1

As shown in Tables 1 and 2, we compared the outlier detection ability of the algorithm under different outlier conditions. Obviously, the higher the outlier level is, the better the detection results are, as the obvious outliers are easily catched. On the other hand, with the increase of outlier count, the detection results are getting worse. Intuitively, extensive outliers have a considerably huge impact on the time series, so it is difficult to distinguish outliers from normal values.

Evaluation of the Predictive Performance
Our method detects the outliers in the time series and revises the parameters of the prediction model to eliminate the effect of abnormal values. In order to illustrate the predictive performance of the modified ARIMA model, we compare the predicted response time and throughput of atomic services with the measured values in the dataset. For comparison, we also conducted experiments based on ARIMA model without outlier detection. Herein sets the outlier level to be medium and the outlier count to be 10. As shown in Fig. 3, compared with ARIMA model without outlier detection, the predicted value obtained by our method can converge to the measured values better. In addition, our method stands out in terms of the root mean square error (RMSE) and mean absolute error (MAE) defined in (16)(17). The details are shown in Table 3.

$$RMSE = \sqrt{\frac{\sum_{i=1}^{n}(actual_i - predicted_i)^2}{n}} \tag{16}$$

$$MAE = \frac{1}{n}\sum_{i=1}^{n}|actual_i - predicted_i| \tag{17}$$

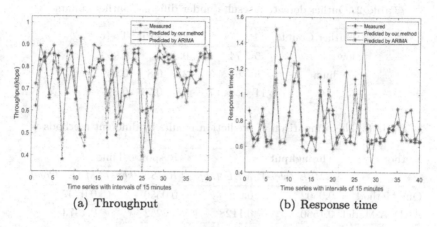

(a) Throughput   (b) Response time

Fig. 3. The comparison of predicted and measured values.

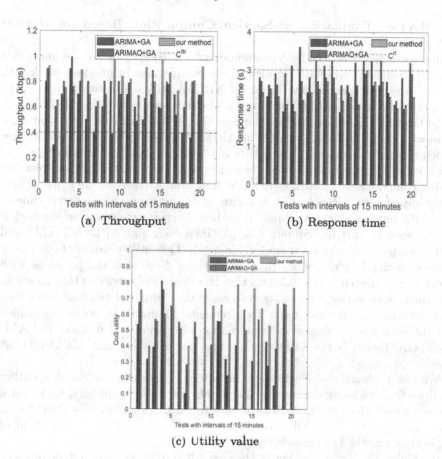

(a) Throughput   (b) Response time

(c) Utility value

Fig. 4. The comparison of composite services' throughput, response time and utility values

Table 2. Outlier detection results under different outlier counts

Outlier Counts	TP	TN	FP	FN	TPR	TNR
low	5	74	1	0	1	0.99
medium	8	67	3	2	0.8	0.96
high	11	58	7	4	0.73	0.89

Table 3. The comparison of prediction results by different methods

Methods	Throughput		Response Time	
	RMSE (kbps)	MAE (kbps)	RMSE (kbps)	MAE (kbps)
Our Method	0.0502	0.0408	0.0550	0.0407
ARIMA Model	0.1560	0.1128	0.2252	0.1573

Effectiveness Evaluation of Service Composition Based on Outlier Detection

In this section, we verify the performance of the composite service generated on the Cybershake template. In view of the comparison in previous work [28], predictive service composition based on ARIMA+GA is obviously superior to other methods in terms of effectiveness and efficiency, so we take ARIMA+GA as the baseline algorithm. And we combine the outlier-tolerable prediction algorithm with traditional GA (denoted as ARIMAO+GA) to verify the advantages of niched genetic algorithm. The results obtained by above three algorithms are indicated in Fig. 4. As can be seen from Fig. 4(a) and (b), the outlier-tolerable service composition algorithms (our method and ARIMAO+GA) are significantly superior to ARIMA+GA in terms of throughput and response time of composite services. Moreover, our niche-based service composition method is also superior to that of ordinary GA (ARIMA+GA and ARIMAO+GA) and rarely violates constraints. Figure 4(c) shows the QoS utility values of composite services obtained by the above three algorithms. Note that the positions with absent bars in the bar graph indicates that the composite service at that time violates the corresponding constraints in terms of throughput or response time, that is, the service cannot meet users' requirements. Similarly, it can be concluded that the outlier-tolerable service composition algorithm (our method and ARIMAO+GA) clearly beats ARIMA+GA, and our method beats ARIMAO+GA as well.

We also evaluate the effectiveness of different algorithms at varying outlier conditions. Considering different outlier levels and outlier numbers, we perform service combinations 30 times in each case to calculate the success rate of each algorithm (i.e., the probability of finding feasible solutions). As shown in of Fig. 5(a), our method achieves better success rates regardless of the outlier levels. As the higher the level of outlier is, the easier it is to detect and handle outliers. Consequently, with the increase of outlier levels, the success rates in outlier-tolerable algorithms(our method and ARIMAO+GA) become better, while the success rates in ARIMA+GA algorithm decrease and is equivalent to the result of random selection. As shown in Fig. 5(b), the success rates of all algorithms decline with the increasing number of outliers. And our algorithm is obviously superior to ARIMAO+GA algorithm and ARIMA+GA algorithm.

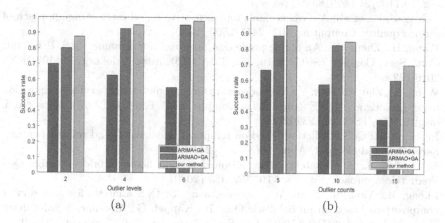

(a)   (b)

Fig. 5. The success rate under different outlier conditions

6 Conclusions

In this work, we consider outliers in service QoS data to be non-neglectable and propose an outlier-tolerable and predictive service composition method. Firstly, a prediction method based on outlier detection is used to process QoS data of candidate services. Besides detecting outliers and eliminating outlier effects, the parameters of ARIMA model are also re-estimated. Then, the predictive data obtained in outlier-tolerable prediction method is exploited into the niched GA which empowered by sharing mechanism and isolation mechanism. The results of case study show that our method is significantly superior to the baseline methods in terms of performance and success rate, which amply demonstrate the necessity of outlier detection and the superiority of niched GA in the process of service composition. In the future, we intend to conduct more comparisons of outlier detection algorithms and try neural network algorithms in the field of outlier-tolerable service composition.

References

1. Wu, Q., Ishikawa, F., Zhu, Q., Shin, D.H.: QoS-aware multigranularity service composition: modeling and optimization. IEEE Trans. Syst. Man Cybern. Syst. 46(11), 1565–1577 (2010). https://doi.org/10.1109/TSMC.2015.2503384
2. Lu, H., Liu, Y., Fei, Z., Guan, C.: An outlier detection algorithm based on cross-correlation analysis for time series dataset. IEEE Access 6, 53593–53610 (2018). https://doi.org/10.1109/ACCESS.2018.2870151

3. Wang, W., Wang, L., Lu, W.: An intelligent QoS identification for untrustworthy web services via two-phase neural networks. IEEE Int. Conf. Web Serv. (ICWS) **2016**, 139–146 (2016). https://doi.org/10.1109/ICWS.2016.26
4. Sun, X., et al.: A fluctuation-aware approach for predictive web service composition. IEEE Int. Conf. Serv. Comput. (SCC) **2018**, 121–128 (2018). https://doi.org/10.1109/SCC.2018.00023
5. Yahyaoui, H., et al.: A novel scalable representative-based forecasting approach of service quality. Computing **102**, 2471–2500 (2020)
6. Wang, H., Zheng, X.: An online prediction approach for dynamic QoS. IEEE Int. Conf. Serv. Comput. (SCC) **2016**, 852–855 (2016). https://doi.org/10.1109/SCC.2016.122
7. Wang, X., Zhu, J., Shen, Y.: Network-aware QoS prediction for service composition using geolocation. IEEE Trans. Serv. Comput. **8**(4), 630–643 (2015). https://doi.org/10.1109/TSC.2014.2320271
8. Li, B., et al.: QoS Prediction based on temporal information and request context. Serv. Oriented Comput. Appl. **15**(3), 231–244 (2021)
9. Li, J., Lin, J.: A probability distribution detection based hybrid ensemble QoS prediction approach. Inf. Sci. **519**, 352–353 (2020)
10. Zheng, H., Yang, J., Zhao, W., Bouguettaya, A.: QoS analysis for web service compositions based on probabilistic QoS. In: Kappel, G., Maamar, Z., Motahari-Nezhad, H.R. (eds.) ICSOC 2011. LNCS, vol. 7084, pp. 47–61. Springer, Heidelberg (2011). https://doi.org/10.1007/978-3-642-25535-9_4
11. Wang, P., Liu, T., Zhan, Y., Du, X.: A Bayesian Nash equilibrium of QoS-aware web service composition. IEEE Int. Conf. Web Serv. (ICWS) **2017**, 676–683 (2017). https://doi.org/10.1109/ICWS.2017.81
12. Hwang, S., Hsu, C., Lee, C.: Service selection for web services with probabilistic QoS. IEEE Trans. Serv. Comput. **8**(3), 467–480 (2015). https://doi.org/10.1109/TSC.2014.2338851
13. Hwang, S., Wang, H., Tang, J., et al.: A probabilistic approach to modeling and estimating the QoS of web-services-based workflows. Inf. Sci. Int. J. **177**(23), 5484–5503 (2007)
14. Yu, Q., Zheng, Z., Wang, H.: Trace norm regularized matrix factorization for service recommendation. In: 2013 IEEE 20th International Conference on Web Services, pp. 34–41 (2013). https://doi.org/10.1109/ICWS.2013.15
15. Zhu, X., et al.: Similarity-maintaining privacy preservation and location-aware low-rank matrix factorization for QoS prediction based web service recommendation. IEEE Trans. Serv. Comput. **14**(3), 889–902 (2021). https://doi.org/10.1109/TSC.2018.2839741
16. Wu, H., Zhang, Z., Luo, J., Yue, K., Hsu, C.H.: Multiple attributes QoS prediction via deep neural model with contexts. IEEE Trans. Serv. Comput. **14**(4), 1084–1096 (2021). https://doi.org/10.1109/TSC.2018.2859986
17. Xu, M., Han, M.: Adaptive elastic echo state network for multivariate time series prediction. IEEE Trans. Cybern. **46**(10), 2173–2183 (2016). https://doi.org/10.1109/TCYB.2015.2467167
18. Rokhman, N.: A survey on mixed-attribute outlier detection methods. CommIT Commun. Inf. Technol. J. **13**(1), 39–44 (2019)
19. Rotman, M., Reis, I., Poznanski, D., Wolf, L.: Detect the unexpected: novelty detection in large astrophysical surveys using fisher vectors. In: Proceedings of 11th International Joint Conference on Knowledge Discovery, Knowledge Engineering, and Knowledge Management, pp. 124–134 (2019)

20. Cook, A. A., Misirli, G., Fan, Z.: Anomaly detection for IoT time-series data: a survey. IEEE Internet Things J. **7**(7), 6481–6494 (2020)

21. Li, Z., Zhao, Y., Hu, X., Botta, N., Ionescu, C., Chen, G.: ECOD: unsupervised outlier detection using empirical cumulative distribution functions. IEEE Transactions on Knowledge and Data Engineering. https://doi.org/10.1109/TKDE.2022.3159580

22. Moustafa, N., Hu, J., Slay, J.: A holistic review of network anomaly detection systems: a comprehensive survey. J. Netw. Comput. Appl. **128**, 33–55 (2019)

23. Gupta, M., Gao, J., Aggarwal, C.C., Han, J.: Outlier detection for temporal data: a survey. IEEE Trans. Knowl. Data Eng. **26**(9), 2250–2267 (2014). https://doi.org/10.1109/TKDE.2013.184

24. Yu, Y., et al.: Time series outlier detection based on sliding window prediction. J. Comput. Appl. **2014**(2), 2217–2220 (2014)

25. Liu, Y., Lu, H.: Outlier detection algorithm based on SOM neural network for spatial series dataset. In: 2018 Tenth International Conference on Advanced Computational Intelligence (ICACI), pp. 162–168 (2018). https://doi.org/10.1109/ICACI.2018.8377600

26. Yousef, W.A., Traor, I., Briguglio, W.: UN-AVOIDS: unsupervised and nonparametric approach for visualizing outliers and invariant detection scoring. IEEE Trans. Inf. Forensics Secur. **16**, 5195–5210 (2021). https://doi.org/10.1109/TIFS.2021.3125608

27. Chen, C., Liu, L.: Joint estimation of model parameters and outlier effects in time series. J. Am. Stat. Assoc. **88**(421), 284C97 (1993). https://doi.org/10.2307/2290724

28. Sun, X., Wang, S., Xia, Y., Zheng, W.: Predictive-trend-aware composition of web services with time-varying quality-of-service. IEEE Access **8**, 1910–1921 (2020). https://doi.org/10.1109/ACCESS.2019.2962703

29. Chen, R., Wang, X.: Situation-aware orchestration of resource allocation and task scheduling for collaborative rendering in IoT visualization. IEEE Transactions on Sustainable Computing. https://doi.org/10.1109/TSUSC.2022.3165016

30. Somasundaram, K.S.G.A., Saranya, A.M.N.N., Prabha, R., Babu, D.V.: A novel hybrid GAACO algorithm for cloud computing using energy aware load balance scheduling. In: 2022 International Conference on Computer Communication and Informatics (ICCCI), pp. 1–5 (2022). https://doi.org/10.1109/ICCCI54379.2022.9740795

31. Zhao, Z., Lee, W.C., Shin, Y., Song, K.: An optimal power scheduling method for demand response in home energy management system. IEEE Trans. Smart Grid **4**(3), 1391–1400 (2013). https://doi.org/10.1109/TSG.2013.2251018

32. Yang, Y., Niu, Y., Lam, H.K.: Sliding-mode control for interval type-2 fuzzy systems: event-triggering WTOD scheme. IEEE Transactions on Cybernetics. https://doi.org/10.1109/TCYB.2022.3163452

33. Ben Othman, M.T., Abdel-Azim, G.: Multiple sequence alignment based on genetic algorithms with new chromosomes representation. In: 2012 16th IEEE Mediterranean Electrotechnical Conference, p. 1030–1033 (2012)

34. Zheng, Z., Zhang, Y., Lyu, M.R.: Investigating QoS of real-world web services. IEEE Trans. Serv. Comput. **7**(1), 32–39 (2014). https://doi.org/10.1109/TSC.2012.34

Towards an Improved Bi-GAN-Based End-to-End One-Class Classifier for Anomaly Detection in Cloud Data-Centers

Jiale Zhao[1], Peng Chen[2($\boxtimes$)], Juan Chen[2], Xianhua Niu[2], and Yunni Xia[1($\boxtimes$)]

[1] School of computers, Chongqing University, Chongqing 400030, China
xiayunni@hotmail.com
[2] School of Computer and Software Engineering, Xihua University, Chengdu 610039, China
chenpeng@mail.xhu.edu.cn

Abstract. With the continuous popularization of cloud computing services, ensuring the stable operation of cloud data-centers has become a hot research issue. Efficient anomaly detection for a running cloud data-center and timely judgment of the cause of anomalies will help to fundamentally improve the reliability of cloud data-center infrastructures. Nevertheless, traditional anomaly identification approaches are challenging to meet the requirements of cloud data-centers with increasingly complex system structures. Due to the low feasibility of labeling data, machine learning methods based on supervised learning also make it difficult to perform efficient anomaly detection in cloud data-centers. This work exploits novel GAN-based generative models and end-to-end one-class classification for optimizing unsupervised anomaly identification. A new Bi-GAN-based Heterogeneous Anomaly-reconstruction One-class Classifier (BG-HA-OC) is developed optimizing a one-class classifier and an anomaly scoring function. The Generator-Encoder-Discriminator Bi-GAN is capable of performing practical anomaly score computation and capturing fine temporal features. In the empirical study, we demonstrate that our proposed framework outperforms its peers upon third-party anomaly detection methods on anomaly benchmarks and synthetic datasets.

Keywords: Anomaly detection · Cloud data-centers · Bidirectional-Generative Adversarial Networks (Bi-GAN) · Unsupervised learning

This work is supported by Science and Technology Program of Sichuan Province under Grant No.2020JDRC0067 and No.2020YFG0326, and Talent Program of Xihua University under Grant No.Z202047, and Postgraduate Scientific Research and Innovation Foundation of Chongqing under Grant No. CYB22064.This work is extended from our previous publication of https://doi.org/10.1093/comjnl/bxac085.

Y. Zhang and L.-J. Zhang (Eds.): ICWS 2022, LNCS 13736, pp. 30–40, 2022.
https://doi.org/10.1007/978-3-031-23579-5_3

1 Introduction

Cloud computing services are products that can be used as service offerings. Including cloud host, cloud space, cloud development, cloud testing, comprehensive products, etc. cloud computing can be divided into Infrastructure as a Service (IaaS), Platform as a Service (PaaS), and Software as a Service (SaaS). In a recent report [1], Gartner, an information technology research and analysis company, noted that the economic benefits generated by IaaS have increased by 40% annually since 2011. The enormous economic benefits of cloud service market have attracted many network security attackers to take advantage of the vulnerabilities of cloud data centers to obtain illegal gains. The most intuitive manifestation of network attacks in cloud data centers is that abnormal data will be generated. Therefore, anomaly detection technology can identify network attacks in cloud data centers. Anomaly detection, by definition, is a technique for identifying abnormal conditions and mining illogical data, also known as outliers. Anomaly detection has always been a very important sub-branch of machine learning. In various artificial intelligence applications such as computer vision, data mining, and Natural Language Processing(NLP), anomaly detection algorithms are general research directions, especially in the era of big data. Humans can no longer process data as fast as machines, so detecting anomalies in data more quickly has become an essential task [1–3].Nevertheless, related works and contributions are still limited in many ways and can be insufficient in handling: 1) Heterogeneity: classes of anomalies can differ from each other and show strong heterogeneity. 2) Rarity: occurrence and distribution of some anomalies can show strong small-sample and few-shot patterns.

Deep Learning(DL) is to learn the inherent laws and representation levels of sample data. The information obtained in these learning processes is of great help to the interpretation of data such as text, images and sounds. It has been achieved in search technology, data mining and other related fields. Regarding anomaly detection, DL detects anomalies by learning representation patterns or anomaly scores through DL networks. Different from traditional distance-oriented methods, one-class classification, probability, or clustering, deep anomaly detection mainly falls into three categories: feature extraction, learning feature representations from normality, and end-to-end anomaly scoring. Generative Adversarial Networks (GAN) [4] framework is proved to be highly potent in various fields, e.g., financial data processing. Nevertheless, GAN's adversarial training models show low efficiency in handling high-dimensional, non-linear, and non-independent data, which are widely existent in the field of anomaly detection.

Instead of relying on normal instances via the mini-max game, in this work, we exploit Generative Adversarial Active Learning (GAAL) [5] for yielding anomalies and propose the Bi-GAN-based Heterogeneous Anomaly-reconstruction One-class Classifier (BG-HA-OC) as the fundamental means of identifying point anomalies within time series. We develop a anomaly scoring

---

[1] http://www.gartner.com/newsroom/id/3354117

function through leveraging a weighted combination of the discriminator's binary cross-entropy and the generator's anomaly reconstruction error. We utilize a Bi-GAN [6] architecture as well for tuning processing efficiency of the reverse mapping of the generator while generating anomalies. It should be noted that the proposed framework aims at identifying point anomalies, specifically outlier or biased instances within time series, rather than those with contextual or collective patterns.

2   Related work

Deep learning has recently been shown to hold incredible promise in various applications. In anomaly detection, intrinsic features are required, and a small number of anomalies need to be used in the full dataset (training/validation). In unsupervised learning, training on an unlabeled training set enables finding the underlying structure of the data set. Consequently, deep-learning-based unsupervised anomaly detection models and algorithms draw considerable research attention and show high capabilities in the field of prediction.

Deep Autoencoding Gaussian Mixture Model (DAGMM) [7] and Long Short-Term Memory (LSTM) En-coder-Decoder [8] show good applicability for data-outlier analysis, through borrowing the model of Auto-Encoder (AE) with adapted constructs of multivariate time series [9–12]. They further utilize a predictability-oriented representation-learning formalism for processing the context-rich information in data series [13–16]. To be specific, they leverage GAN-based [4] procedures, due to their capabilities of capturing deep representations of samples by leveraging a mini-max game. Recently, a novel Anomaly detection with Generative Adversarial Networks (Ano-GAN) [17] was proposed for learning latent factors and thus exploiting outliers hidden in latent space. Some forms of residual between the real instance and the generated instance are then defined as anomaly score. EGAN [18], fast AnoGAN [19] and GANomaly [20] fall into this category as well.

3   Our Method: BG-HA-OC

3.1   Problem Formulation

As GAN-based generation methods do, generator G's and discriminator D's parameters are updated based on D's output up to Nash equilibrium. Specifically, discriminator D is trained for high sensitivity in assigning correct labels to real or fake data instances. On the other hand, after sufficient iterations, the generator G is simultaneously made to deceive the discriminator as subtly as possible. It is conceivable that generator G will be able to understand better the hidden distribution of the training inputs and yield real samples. In theory, in a typical GAN model, the generator takes randomly generated noise as inputs. It can directly yield informative potential abnormal instances with the guidance of the discriminator. For such spurious exception generation, exception scoring can be used. Therefore, the discriminator identifies anomalies according to anomaly scores through analyzing a partition bounds that separates underlying anomalies out of normal samples. It is assumed that the group distribution of the dataset is supposed to be unbalanced between abnormal and normal ones.

To be more concrete, for a data instance x, the detection model is supposed to identify an instance z from latent feature space of the generative network G in a way that the corresponding generated instance $G(z)$ and x diverge to each other. Because the use of latent space helps to learn potentially key features of the training dataset, exceptions are with reduced similarity to their generated counterparts. Consequently, a GAN is first trained with the following conventional objective:

$$\min_{\Theta_G} \max_{\Theta_D} V(D,G) = \mathrm{E}_{x \sim px}[\log[D(x)] + \mathrm{E}_{x \sim pz}[\log[1 - D(G(z))] \qquad (1)$$

where G and D are with parameters of Θ_G and Θ_D, and V denotes the value function of mini-max game. For every x, to identify its corresponding z, a residual loss and a discrimination-loss one are employed to guide the search.

The search is initialized with a randomly sampled z and updates z according to the gradients by the loss function:

$$s_x = (1 - \alpha)\ell_R(X, Z_\gamma) + \alpha \ell_{fm}(X, Z_\gamma) \qquad (2)$$

The anomaly score can thus be defined according to the similarity between x and z derived at the last step $\gamma*$:

$$s_x = (1 - \alpha)\ell_R(X, Z_{\gamma*}) + \alpha \ell_{fm}(X, Z_{\gamma*}) \qquad (3)$$

With the help of the mini-max game D is able to learn to be a one-class classifier and thus acquire improved discrimination capability. In this sense, $D(G(z))$ serves as τ in the detection model.

Based on the two GAN-relevant methods, the two difficulties as mentioned earlier are transferred into two key problems: 1) How to define a computational efficient anomaly scoring function. 2) How to conduct simultaneous temporal representation capture and one-class classifier for complex logs of multivariate time series. To perform effective anomaly detection in the real-time operation of data infrastructure, we should handle them reasonably. If it is too long, anomaly detection is not effective enough for real-time operation. However, if a short interval, like less than 1 minute, infrastructure provisioning like VM initialization may not even finish. Therefore, we must take time cost into account.

3.2 BG-HA-OC Architecture

To combine the computing power of GAN's generator and discriminator architecture, in Figure 1, we develop a novel model, BG-HA-OC. In this architecture, the discriminator D serves as a one-class classifier, while the generator G reports instance refactoring of exceptions. G yields false anomalies from the noise in the

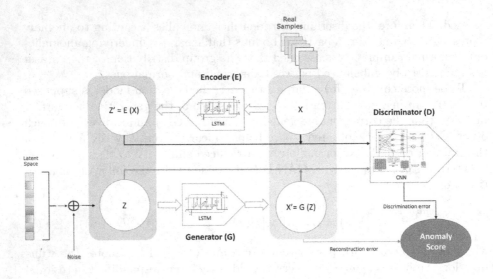

Fig. 1. BG-HA-OC architecture

latent space and D distinguishes the resulting anomalies out of normal ones. With adversarial training D is tamed as a robust one-class classifier able to learn the representation of exceptions when the discriminator is with sufficient sensitivity to allocate the correct labels. Consequently, the reconstruction error of G accounts for the anomaly score, as well as the direct binary cross-entropy from D, i.e., $D(G(z))$. The reconstruction error represents the residual between the test samples and the reconstructed ones.

Thus, the anomaly scoring function is supposed to be designed with a synthesis of binary cross-entropy from D and the anomaly reconstruction error from G:

$$s_x = \alpha \ell_{OC}(X) - (1 - \alpha)\ell_{AR}(X) \tag{4}$$

where ℓ_{OC} denotes the one-class classification error and ℓ_{AR} anomaly reconstruction error.

3.3 Bi-GAN-based Anomaly Score Estimation

This section deals with the calculation of anomaly score. The above-mentioned reconstruction error is calculated according to the gap between the reconstructed samples and the actual ones. Nevertheless, this can't be done through reverse mapping since G corresponds to the mapping from the latent space to the real data one. Inspired by the concept of Bi-GAN [6], the encoder-generator-discriminator structure of Bi-GAN is adopted to update the overall architecture accordingly so that the E, G and D can be trained adversarially E can thus be interpreted as a reverse mapping from the real data space to the latent one, for reduced model complexity. In this way, $G(E(x))$ is treated as the reconstructed instance with the real input one:

$$\ell_{AR}(X) = \|x - G(E(X))\|_1 \tag{5}$$

With Bi-GAN, the overall mini-max game as follows:

$$\begin{array}{c} \min_{\Theta_E} \max_{\Theta_G} \max_{\Theta_D} \mathrm{E}_{x \sim px} \left[\mathrm{E}_{x \sim pE(\cdot|x)} \log[D(x,z)] \right] \\ + \mathrm{E}_{x \sim pz} \left[\mathrm{E}_{x \sim pG(\cdot|z)} [\log(1 - D(x,z))] \right] \end{array} \tag{6}$$

3.4   Heterogeneous Generator and Discriminator

This section deals with the construction of the generator and discriminator of Bi-GAN. We employ LSTM and CNN as the underlying model for constructing the generator and discriminator, respectively. G takes a sequence from a random latent space as the input to generate false anomalies. It then forward generated exceptions to D, which combines the generated exceptions with the normal training data sequence as a generic one-class classifier. By doing so, Bi-GAN is with better heterogeneity and thus makes full use of the computing power of LSTM and CNN. Note that, the improved heterogeneity helps to mitigate over fitting as well.

4   Evaluation

To validate the performance of the proposed anomaly detection method, we conduct experiments using six datasets of two categories, which are illustrated in Fig. 2.

1) Open anomaly detection datasets: This category comprises the "vertebral" and "optdigits" datasets. They are featured by small sample sizes and ranged anomaly rates.
2) Synthetic datasets: This category comprises four synthetic datasets , namely Synthetic 1–4, which are generated by using the PyOD[2] toolset.

The experimental environment is based on a single server with Intel Xeon Processor 4 Core Skylake CPU, an Nvidia T4 GPU and Anaconda 3, Python 3.8, Cuda 11.1 tools

We consider Precision, Recall, Processing time and $F1$ as the metrics. We use K-Nearest Neighbour (KNN) [21], Angle-Based Outlier Detection (ABOD) [22], Isolation Forest (IF) [23] and Auto-Encoder (AE) [7] as the peers. As to the GAN-based methods, we use Efficient GAN (EGAN) [18] and Generative Adversarial Active Learning (GAAL) method [5] as peers as well.

As shown in Fig. 3. In the "vertebral" benchmark, BG-HA-OC shows the best performance, compared with the second-winner MO GAAL, BG-HA-OC is

---

[2] https://pyod.readthedocs.io/en/latest/pyod.html

Dataset	Abbr.	Variables	Samples	Type	Anomaly Percentage
vertebral	Ve	6	240	Benchmark	12.50%
optdigits	Op	64	5216	Benchmark	2.88%
Synthetic 1	S1	200	33000	Synthetic	15.00%
Synthetic 2	S2	100	12000	Synthetic	5.00%
Synthetic 3	S3	50	4000	Synthetic	5.00%
Synthetic 4	S4	50	18000	Synthetic	15.00%

Fig. 2. General information of six test datasets

Dataset	Method	Precision	Recall	F1	Duration	Rank
vertebral	KNN	0.4302	0.4405	0.4353	**0.0186**	7
	ABOD	0.4318	0.4524	0.4419	0.0559	6
	IF	0.4286	0.4286	0.4286	0.3529	8
	AE	<u>0.4634</u>	<u>0.4583</u>	<u>0.4613</u>	2.8225	4
	SO GAAL	0.4686	0.4642	0.4662	<u>3.5628</u>	3
	MO GAAL	0.486	0.4881	0.4866	21.8672	2
	EGAN	0.4598	0.4464	0.4517	3.5947	5
	BG-HA-OC	**0.5767**	**0.5436**	**0.5519**	9.0861	1
optdigits	KNN	0.4865	0.4579	0.47	2.7611	6
	ABOD	0.4928	0.4738	0.4749	3.3089	5
	IF	<u>0.5105</u>	<u>0.5361</u>	<u>0.5032</u>	**0.9948**	1
	AE	0.486	0.4509	0.4658	7.2231	8
	SO GAAL	0.503	0.5093	0.4948	<u>13.6825</u>	3
	MO GAAL	**0.5044**	**0.516**	**0.4927**	131.3917	2
	EGAN	0.4863	0.4556	0.4686	15.3933	7
	BG-HA-OC	0.4947	0.4834	0.4822	41.5841	4

[*] The best result among KNN, ABOD, IF, and AE is underlined.
[*] Double underline is for the best among 4 GAN-based methods.
[*] The overall best for each metric is bold.

Fig. 3. Simulative results

Dataset	Method	Precision	Recall	F1	Duration	Rank
Sample=33000 Dim=200 CR=0.15	KNN	0.9724	0.8344	0.8866	451.7546	2
	ABOD	0.9717	0.83	0.883	455.0937	3
	IF	0.9712	0.8267	0.8803	**13.6794**	4
	AE	0.9694	0.8156	0.8712	75.126	5
	SO GAAL	0.4958	0.4972	0.4929	204.8572	6
	MO GAAL	0.481	0.4868	0.4814	2304.483	7
	EGAN	0.4157	0.4351	0.4252	248.5142	8
	BG-HA-OC	**0.9736**	**0.8422**	**0.8928**	427.9677	1
Sample=12000 Dim=100 CR=0.05	KNN	0.7451	0.9726	0.8149	26.9207	3
	ABOD	0.7273	0.9684	0.7962	27.3808	5
	IF	0.7427	0.9721	0.8124	**1.7035**	4
	AE	0.7463	0.9729	0.8161	20.4199	2
	SO GAAL	0.5612	0.6124	0.5746	56.0444	7
	MO GAAL	0.5763	0.6503	0.5949	504.5886	6
	EGAN	0.472	0.4439	0.4576	57.8765	8
	BG-HA-OC	**0.766**	**0.9768**	**0.8354**	123.7224	1
Sample=4000 Dim=50 CR=0.05	KNN	**0.7809**	**0.9795**	**0.8492**	1.5843	1
	ABOD	0.7551	0.9747	0.8249	2.0324	3
	IF	0.7525	0.9742	0.8223	**0.6736**	4
	AE	0.7427	0.9721	0.8123	7.4666	5
	SO GAAL	0.5897	0.6921	0.6136	16.9357	7
	MO GAAL	0.694	0.8774	0.7488	132.9787	6
	EGAN	0.4714	0.4342	0.4521	15.8845	8
	BG-HA-OC	0.7688	0.9774	0.8381	37.7779	2
Sample=18000 Dim=50 CR=0.15	KNN	0.9674	0.8022	0.8599	23.963	6
	ABOD	0.9713	0.8278	0.8812	25.8787	2
	IF	0.9708	0.8244	0.8785	**1.7982**	3
	AE	0.97	0.8189	0.8739	25.2651	4
	SO GAAL	0.5061	0.5042	0.5017	74.4308	8
	MO GAAL	0.5584	0.5359	0.539	793.8951	7
	EGAN	0.9694	0.8159	0.8712	77.9439	5
	BG-HA-OC	**0.974**	**0.8444**	**0.8945**	166.3911	1

* The best result among KNN, ABOD, IF, and AE is underlined.
* Double underline is for the best among 4 GAN-based methods.
* The overall best for each metric is bold.

Fig. 1. Experiment results for synthetic datasets

9.07% higher in Precision, 5.55% higher in Recall and 6.53% higher in F1, the average runtime was reduced by 12.7811 s seconds. On the "optdigits" benchmark, the GAN-based methods are all average or even below average.

As shown in Fig. 4. BG-HA-OC provides the best metrics for three of the four datasets, demonstrating that the proposed BG-HA-OC can achieve better robustness. Although BG-HA-OC takes longer, it achieves better performance, which we consider acceptable.

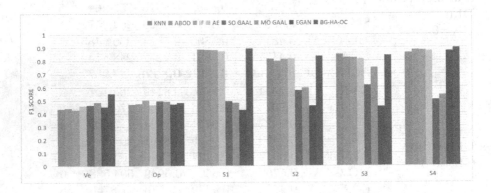

Fig. 5. The overall F1 Scores for all the compared anomaly detection methods on the given six test datasets. Ve and Op for the two benchmarks while S1-S4 for the 4 synthetic datasets.

Overall, as shown in Fig. 5 BG-HA-OC outperformed the popular unsupervised detection methods for most situations. To be more specific, among all these 6 test datasets, the proposed BG-HA-OC ranks no.1 for four times, and for remain two datasets, it ranks no.2 and no.4.

5   Conclusion

This paper proposes a new anomaly detection method, BG-HA-OC, which achieves the best performance on anomaly benchmarks and synthetic datasets compared to several state-of-the-art methods for multivariate time series point anomaly detection. metrics and rankings. Further experiments show that BG-HA-OC has strong robustness. In future work, we plan to further investigate the introduction of multi-classification in the discriminator with the capability of anomaly diagnosis and interpretation, which is crucial for operating such cloud data centers.

References

1. Mao, J., Wang, T., Jin, C., Zhou, A.: Feature grouping-based outlier detection upon streaming trajectories. IEEE Trans. Knowl. Data Eng. **29**(12), 2696–2709 (2017)

2. Fiore, U., De Santis, A., Perla, F., Zanetti, P., Palmieri, F.: Using generative adversarial networks for improving classification effectiveness in credit card fraud detection. Inf. Sci. **479**(1), 448–455 (2019)
3. Zhang, L., et al.: Probabilistic-mismatch anomaly detection: do one's medications match with the diagnoses. In: 2016 IEEE 16th International Conference on Data Mining (ICDM), pp. 659–668 (2016)
4. Goodfellow, I., et al.: Generative adversarial nets. In: Advances in Neural Information Processing Systems, vol. 27, no. 1 (2014)
5. Liu, Y., et al.: Generative adversarial active learning for unsupervised outlier detection. IEEE Trans. Knowl. Data Eng. **32**(8), 1517–1528 (2019)
6. Donahue, J., Krähenbühl, P., Darrell, T.: Adversarial feature learning. In: 5th International Conference on Learning Representations(ICLR), pp. 1–18 (2016)
7. Zong, B., et al.: Deep autoencoding gaussian mixture model for unsupervised anomaly detection. In: International Conference on Learning Representations, pp. 1–19 (2018)
8. Habler, E., Shabtai, A.: Using LSTM encoder-decoder algorithm for detecting anomalous ads-b messages. Comput. Secur. **78**(1), 155–173 (2018)
9. Gao, H., Qiu, B., Barroso, R. J. D., Hussain, W., Xu, Y., Wang, X.: TSMAE: a novel anomaly detection approach for internet of things time series data using memory-augmented autoencoder. IEEE Transactions on Network Science and Engineering, pp. 1–14 (2022)
10. Zhang, C., et al.: A deep neural network for unsupervised anomaly detection and diagnosis in multivariate time series data. Proc. AAAI Conf. Artif. Intell. **33**(1), 1409–1416 (2019)
11. Luo, W., Liu, W., Gao, S.: Remembering history with convolutional LSTM for anomaly detection. In: 2017 IEEE International Conference on Multimedia and Expo (ICME), pp. 439–444 (2017)
12. Ding, K., Li, J., Bhanushali, R., Liu, H.: Deep anomaly detection on attributed networks. In: Proceedings of the 2019 SIAM International Conference on Data Mining, pp. 594–602 (2019)
13. Hsieh, J.-T., Liu, B., Huang, D.-A., Fei-Fei, L.F., Niebles, J.C.: Learning to decompose and disentangle representations for video prediction. In: Advances in Neural Information Processing Systems, vol. 31, no. 1 (2018)
14. Liao, B., et al.: Deep sequence learning with auxiliary information for traffic prediction. In: Proceedings of the 24th ACM SIGKDD International Conference on Knowledge Discovery Data Mining, pp. 537–546 (2018)
15. Gao, H., Xiao, J., Yin, Y., Liu, T., Shi, J.: A mutually supervised graph attention network for few-shot segmentation: the perspective of fully utilizing limited samples. IEEE Transactions on Neural Networks and Learning Systems (2022)
16. Xu, R., Cheng, Y., Liu, Z., Xie, Y., Yang, Y.: Improved long short-term memory based anomaly detection with concept drift adaptive method for supporting IoT services. Futur. Gener. Comput. Syst. **112**(1), 228–242 (2020)
17. Schlegl, T., Seeböck, P., Waldstein, S.M., Schmidt-Erfurth, U., Langs, G.: Unsupervised anomaly detection with generative adversarial networks to guide marker discovery. In: International Conference on Information Processing in Medical Imaging, pp. 146–157 (2017)
18. Zenati, H , Foo, C.S., Lecouat, B., Manek, G., Chandrasekhar, V.R.: Efficient GaN-based anomaly detection. In: 6th International Conference on Learning Representations(ICLR), pp. 1–13 (2018)

19. Schlegl, T., Seeböck, P., Waldstein, S.M., Langs, G., Schmidt-Erfurth, U.: f-AnoGaN: fast unsupervised anomaly detection with generative adversarial networks. Med. Image Anal. **54**(1), 30–44 (2019)
20. Akcay, S., Atapour-Abarghouei, A., Breckon, T.P.: Ganomaly: semi-supervised anomaly detection via adversarial training. In: Asian Conference on Computer Vision, pp. 622–637 (2018)
21. Angiulli, F., Pizzuti, C.: Fast outlier detection in high dimensional spaces. In: European Conference on Principles of Data Mining and Knowledge Discovery, pp. 15–27 (2002)
22. Kriegel, H., Schubert, M., Zimek, A.: Angle-based outlier detection in high-dimensional data. In: Proceedings of the 14th ACM SIGKDD International Conference on Knowledge Discovery and Data Mining, pp. 444–452 (2008)
23. Liu, F., Ting, K., Zhou, Z.: Isolation forest. In: 2008 Eighth IEEE International Conference on Data Mining, pp. 413–422 (2008)

A Novel Approach for User Demand-aware Data Center Construction and Service Consolidation

Yifei Lv[1], Kunyin Guo[1], Yunni Xia[1(✉)], Yin Li[2], Yong Ma[3], Fan Li[4], Linchengxi Zeng[5], Qinglan Peng[6], and Tingyan Long[1]

[1] College of Computer Science, Chongqing University, Chongqing 400030, China
xiayunni@hotmail.com
[2] Guangzhou Institute of Software Application Technology, Guangzhou 510000, China
[3] School of Computers and Information, Jiangxi Normal University, Nanchang 330022, China
[4] Key Laboratory of Fundamental Synthetic Vision Graphics and Image Science for National Defense, Sichuan University, Chengdu 610000, China
[5] Mashang Consumer Finance Company Ltd. (MSCF), Chongqing, China
[6] School of Artificial Intelligence, Henan University, Kaifeng 475001, China

Abstract. The recent intensifying computational demands from multi-nationals enterprises have motivated the magnification for large complicated cloud data centers (DCs) to handle business, monetary, Internet and commercial applications of different enterprises. A cloud data center encompasses thousands of physical server nodes arranged in racks along with network, storage, and other equipment that entails an extensive amount of power to process different processes and amenities required by business firms. More and more cloud data centers are turning for adapting to dynamics of user demands and reducing operational cost. Therefore, in this paper, we propose a user demand-aware (UDA) method for servers selection and a modified adaptive large neighbourhood search (MALNS) algorithm for dynamic service consolidation. Experiments based on real-world datasets demonstrate our approach outperformed conventional strategies in terms of multiple metrics.

Keywords: Cloud computing · Data center construction · Service consolidation · Cost · Resource utilization · Heuristic algorithms

1 Introduction

Cloud data centers are well-known powerful computational infrastructures that provide flexible, efficient, and cost-effective information technology solutions for

This work is supported by Graduate Research and Innovation Foundations of Chongqing, China under Grant Nos.CYS21062 and CYS22112. This work is supported by National Science Foundations under Grant Nos. 6217206 and 62162036.

multinationals to offer improved and enhanced quality of business services to end-users. They are suited for powering versatile types of applications and computational scenariosg [1–7]. A significant number of nowadays data centers are equipped with thousands or even more servers. This results in huge monetary cost and incurs various issues for budget efficiency.

Cost of data centers usually comprises two parts: hardware cost and energy one. Hardware cost refers to the expense of purchasing or renting hardware and computational/communication/storage facilities. In practice, the cloud providers need to purchase servers to satisfy the user demand, but the resource demands of users never perfectly match resource availability. A discrepancy and inappropriate purchase strategy can lead to high monetary waste and low resource utilization, especially when cloud providers have to pay for a large resource package but only a part of it is actually used. On the other hand, handling energy cost is not a easy task as well. Due to the discrepancy between resource demands and resource availability, DCs have to turn on a fresh service process, usually in terms of a virtual machine (VM) or a cloud node for accommodating fragmented resource demands, which leads to high energy consumption and further resource fragmentation.

In order to deal with the resource and demand heterogeneity, we formulate the resource constraint-aware service placement and consolidation problem as a type of Vector Bin packing problem, which is known to be NP-hard. Thus, an efficient algorithm capable of yielding high-quality solutions with low DC cost as the optimization objective is in high need in practice. As the number of requests for service resources increases, the cloud provider needs to purchase new servers to expand the DCs. However, it's difficult to predict the amount of resources requested by users in advance and thus the specific type of servers to be purchased is hard to decide. As risks of both over sufficient and insufficient resource of servers do exist, an user demand-aware purchasing strategy is meaningful. On the other hand, idle resources releases at runtime can be high fragmented and thus hard to utilized. In this view, a smart consolidation strategy for consolidating fragmented resources is in high need as well.

For the above purposes, in this paper:

- We propose a user-demand-aware server selection method for reducing the hardware cost.
- We propose a modified adaptive large neighbourhood search algorithm for dynamically adjusting the migration strategies for reducing energy cost.
- We conduct extensive simulations and show that our proposed method outperforms its peers in terms of resource utilization and cost.

The rest of this article is organized as follows: Sect. 2 reports the related works. Section 3 describes the system model and problems formulation. Section 4 presents the algorithm. Section 5 visually conceptualizes the results of the experimental and its performance comparison. Finally, Sect. 6 offers the conclusion and further studies.

2   Relate work

Service consolidation is widely believed to be a effective means of tuning performance and reducing energy consumption of distributed systems. Extensive research efforts were paid in this direction through using varying types of optimization strategies, heuristics and intelligent algorithms [8].

Beloglazov et al. [9] regarded the service integration problem as a Bin Packing problem, and proposed an energy-aware BFD strategy for energy optimization. Fu et al. [10] introduced a host selection and service placement method by estimating the minimum correlation coefficient between the CPU availability and requirement. However, this method considered CPU as the only resource constraint. Nithiya et al. [11] proposed a service placement algorithm by adopting a Fuzzu soft set (FSS) model capable of taking into account both CPU and memory as resource constraints. It uses the minimum correlation coefficient as an evaluation index when selecting hosts. Alsadie et al. [12] proposed a dynamic threshold algorithm based on fuzzy detection method that can adaptively migrate virtual machines from the host under low or over load state. Wang et al. [13] developed a bionic algorithm for improving the resource utilization rate of DC. It calculates the matching degree of VM and the host as the basis of consolidating the VM cluster.

Recently, energy efficiency is considered as another important optimization objective for service consolidation as well. Li et al. [14] proposed the discrete differential evolution algorithm for searching for the global optimal solutions for service consolidation. Farahnakian et al. [15] proposed a regression model for predicting the future usage of resources. Wu et al. [16] developed a improved genetic algorithm for reducing the energy consumption of the DC. Khan et al. [17] proposed an online manner for placing virtual machines while minimizing energy consumption and migration count. Xiao et al. [18] proposed an alliance game theory based method and a merger-and-split strategy for service consolidation in heterogeneous clouds. Wu et al. [19] developed a electricity price-aware algorithm for offline and online lowest electricity expenditures. Mapetu et al. [20] proposed a dynamic service consolidation approach-based load balancing for minimizing the trade-off between energy consumption and SLA violations. Mahdhi et al. [21] proposed a VM consolidation method based on estimates of service migration traffic. It aims at optimizing migrations count and energy consumption. Haghshenas et al. [22] proposed a regression-based and predictive approach for saving energy in DCs. Li et al. [23] proposed a prediction-based virtual machine placement algorithm method through conducting migrations from highly-loaded machines towards ones with low loads.

3   System Model and Problem Formulation

In this section, we give the system model and problem statement. **Table** 1 illustrates the symbols and their meaning.

Table 1. Symbols and comments

Symbol	Description
c_k	The CPUs of the k-th type of server
d_j	The date of pending request r_j
e_k	The daily energy cost of the k-th type of server
ec_l	The daily energy cost of DC of the lth day
$f_{i,j}$	A boolean indicator of whether request r_j is on server s_i before migration
$\hat{f}_{i,j}$	A boolean indicator of whether request r_j is on server s_i after migration
h_k	The hardware cost of the k-th type of server
hc	The total hardware cost of DC
m	The number of types of servers
m_k	The memory of the k-th type of server
n	The number of users' requests
p	The number of procured servers in DC
r_j	The j-th pending request
rc_j	The CPU demands of request r_j
rm_j	The memory demands of request r_j
s_i	The i-th procured servers is DC
sc_i	The capacity of CPU of server s_i
sm_i	The capacity of memory of server s_i
S	The set of procured servers
t_j	A boolean indicator of whether release or apply for a VM
tec	The total energy cost of DC
u	The max number of daily migration count
x_k	The number servers with the k-th type be purchased
y	The operating time of DC by days

3.1 System Model

Servers Cluster Construction Model. There is a sequence of user requests that are occurring over a period of time, $r_j, j = (1, 2, 3, ...n)$ is used to donate the j-th request. r_j is described by a four-tuple $\{t_j, rc_j, rm_j, d_j\}$, where t_j is an indicator of whether to release or apply for a service, in terms of a VM, rc_j and rm_j is the number of CPUs and memory of the VM, d_j represents the occurrence day of this request. We needs to purchase servers for carrying these requests and there are m types of available servers to select. We use c_k, m_k, h_k to denote the number of CPUs, the number of memory, the hardware cost of servers with the k-th type, where $k = (1, 2, 3, ..., m)$. x_k ($x_k \geq 0$) denotes the number of procured server with k-th type. The total hardware cost of DC is calculated as follows:

$$hc = \sum_{k=1}^{m} x_k \cdot h_k \tag{1}$$

(1) is supposed to follow the following constraint, the total amount of resources owned by the DC should be greater than that requested by the user.

$$\sum_{k=1}^{m} c_k > \sum_{j=1}^{n} rc_j \tag{2a}$$

$$\sum_{k=1}^{m} m_k > \sum_{j=1}^{n} rm_j \tag{2b}$$

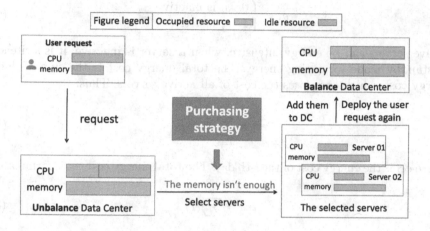

Fig. 1. Purchasing strategy

VM Placement and Service Consolidation Model. In this stage, the procured servers are used for constructing the infrastructure of DC. For VM placement and consolidation, we use S to denote the set of servers in DC, $S = \{s_1, s_2, ..., s_i\}(1 \leq i \leq p)$, where s_i is the i-th server and l is the number of servers. s_i is a three-tuple $\{sc_i, sm_i, se_i\}$, where sc_i is the capacity of CPU, sm_i is the capacity of memory, se_i is the daily energy cost of s_i. We use $f_{i,j}$ to denote a boolean indicator of whether request r_j is on server s_i. It is formulated as:

$$f_{i,j} = \begin{cases} 1, & r_j \in s_i \\ 0, & r_j \notin s_i \end{cases} \tag{3}$$

Each request can be dispatched to only one server, and thus:

$$\sum_{i=1}^{l} f_{i,j} = 1 \tag{4}$$

For each server s_i, its resource allocated are bounded by its availability and thus:

$$\sum rc_j \leq sc_i \quad \forall r_j \in s_i \tag{5a}$$

$$\sum rm_j \leq sm_i \quad \forall r_j \in s_i \tag{5b}$$

The energy consumption of the server is related to the load status of it. In this paper, we divide the servers into active status (with load) and inactive status (without load). a_i is a boolean indicator of whether s_i is active:

$$a_i = \begin{cases} 0, & s_i \text{ is inactive} \\ 1, & s_i \text{ is active} \end{cases} \tag{6}$$

Active servers can be energy intensive, when a server is inactive, it is switched to standby mode for saving energy. The total energy cost is the sum of daily energy cost, which comprises the cost of all active servers. Thus:

$$ec_l = \sum_{i=1}^{l} a_i \cdot se_i \tag{7}$$

where ec_l is the energy cost of the l-th day. The total energy cost tec is formulated as:

$$tec = \sum_{l=1}^{y} ec_l \tag{8}$$

where y is the time that the DC has been running. According to [24] the energy cost is positively correlated with the number of migration. Due to the fact that migrations themselves are energy-requiring and time requiring, the maximum number of migration per day is bounded by 5 % of the number of active VMs in DC. We consider the number of migrations per day , u, as another constraint:

$$u = \sum_{i=1}^{l} \sum_{j=1}^{n} \frac{|f_{i,j} - \tilde{f}_{i,j}|}{2} \quad (u \leq nav \times 5\%) \tag{9}$$

where $\tilde{f}_{i,j}$ represents a boolean indicator of whether request r_j is on server s_i after migration. nav the number of active VMs in DC.

3.2   Problem Formulation

Based on above analysis, the optimization objective is thus to deploy n requests into m servers with as-low-as-possible cost. The problem is formulated as follows:

$$min \quad \sum_{k=1}^{m} x_k \cdot h_k + \sum_{d=1}^{y} ec_d$$

$$s.t. \quad \sum_{\forall r_j \in s_i} rc_j \leqslant sc_i \tag{10a}$$

$$\sum_{\forall r_j \in s_i} rm_j \leqslant sm_i \tag{10b}$$

$$\sum_{k=1}^{m} c_k > \sum_{j=1}^{n} rc_j \tag{10c}$$

$$\sum_{k=1}^{m} m_k > \sum_{j=1}^{n} rm_j \tag{10d}$$

$$0 < i < l; 0 < j < n; 0 < k < m; \tag{10e}$$

The objective is thus to get lower cost reduce cost with the constraints of (10a-10e). In particular, (10a) and (10b) ensure that the resources of VMs deployed on each server don't exceed those available; (10c) and (10d) ensure that the available resources for all users is exceed those of all requests.

The problem can be relaxed to a two-dimensional vector bin packing problem, which has been proved to be NP-hard in [25–27].

4   Proposed Algorithm

4.1   Servers Cluster Construction Strategy

The goal of servers cluster construction is to reduce the hardware cost by an efficient purchasing strategy. As a first step, we need to identify the servers. We build a multi-variable linear regression model to calculate the cost-effectiveness of the servers, the equation of hardware cost h_k , CPU c_k and memory m_k of the k-th server is:

$$h_k = b_1 \cdot c_k + b_2 \cdot m_k + b_0 \tag{11}$$

where b_1 and b_2 is the regression coefficients, b_0 is a constant for error correction.

To deal with the gap between resource demand and availability, we propose a User Demand-Aware algorithm (UDA). As shown in Fig. 1, when there are insufficient resources in the DC and a new server needs to be purchased, a suitable server is procured according to **Algorithm** 1, which shows its pseudo codes. An empty set S_c is initialized in line 5, which is use for maintaining the candidate servers that selected by the first greedy selection. Line 6–?? conduct the candidate servers according to the urgent resource. Line 23–24 conduct the server selection according to their cost-effectiveness. Line 25 returns the selected server.

Algorithm 1. User Demand Awared Algorithm

Require:
1: rc: The available CPUs remaining in DC
2: rm: The available memories remaining in DC
3: tc: The total CPUs requested by users
4: tm: The total memories requested by users
Ensure: x_k
5: **Init:** Set S_c as the candidate set
6: $g_r = \frac{rc}{rm}$: The ratio of remaining CPU to memory
7: $g_t = \frac{tc}{tm}$: The ratio of CPU to memory requested by users
8: **if** $g_r > g_t$ **then**
9:    **for** each type of server **do**
10:        calculate the ratio of CPU to memory: $g_k = \frac{c_k}{m_k}$
11:        **if** $g_k < g_r$ **then**
12:            Add the server to the candidate set S_c
13:        **end if**
14:    **end for**
15: **else**
16:    **for** each type of server **do**
17:        calculate the ratio of CPU to memory: $g_k = \frac{c_k}{m_k}$
18:        **if** $g_k \geq g_r$ **then**
19:            Add the server to the candidate set S_c
20:        **end if**
21:    **end for**
22: **end if**
23: Calculate the price performanc of the servers in S_c by (12)
24: Select the k-th type of server with the best price performance from S_c
25: $x_k = x_k + 1$

4.2 Service Consolidation Algorithm

In this stage, under-utilized servers are consolidated. As an example in Fig. 2, resource usage in different servers are different. Thus, the consolidation can be applied to create idle servers and transfer hot pages to other servers for optimizing the resource utilization.

The consolidation strategy consists of emigrating VMs from source servers and immigrating VMs to target servers. We propose a modified adaptive large neighbourhood search algorithm (MALNS) to yield the emigration and immigration schedules.

MALNS: In the proposed algorithm, the destroy operators are used to delete the mappings between VMs and servers, the repair operators are used to build new mappings.

Destroy operators:

- Operator 1: Servers are migrated based on the amount of idle resources and the one with most idle resources is migrated from at first.
- Operator 2: Servers are migrated based on the number of the VMs that they host, the server with least VMs is migrated from first.

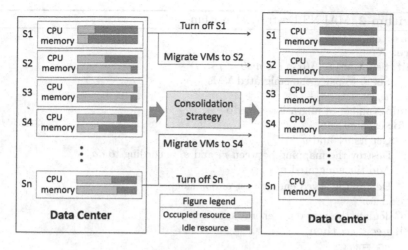

Fig. 2. VM consolidation strategy

– Operator 3: Servers are migrated according to the resources gap $|g_r - g_t|$. The server with highest $|g_r - g_t|$ is migrated from first.

Repair operators:

– Operator 1: Target servers are sorted based on the number of CPUs.
– Operator 2: Target servers are sorted based on the number of memory.
– Operator 3: Target servers are sorted based on the total remaining resources.
– Operator 4: Target servers are sorted based on the unit cost which is calculated as:

$$\frac{b_2}{b_1} \cdot rc_j + rm_j \tag{12}$$

The destroy operators are do_p, where $p = (1, 2, 3, ..., z)$ and z is the number of destroy operators. The weight of do_p is w_p and $\sum_{p=1}^{z} w_p = 1$. It is updated during the pre-migrations. **Algorithm** 2 shows the process of proposed algorithm. Lines 1–2 deal the mapping between VMs and servers. Line 3 implies that every do_p has the same weight and the initial number of migrations. Lines 4–10 perform the emigration VMs from DC according to operator do_p and place the emigrated VMs. The new daily energy cost of DC is updated after each pre-migration. Lines 11–13 show the method for updating the weight of each operator. The operators are viewed as high-quality operator and ordinary ones according to their energy cost savings. Their weights consist of basic weight and temporary weight. The temporary weight are updated by (13) and (14) respectively:

$$\tilde{w}_t = \tilde{w} + (1 - \tilde{w}) \cdot \frac{\tilde{e}}{\sum_{i=1}^{z} e'_p} \tag{13}$$

where $\tilde{w}_t$ is the updated temporary weight of the optimal operator. $\tilde{w}_t$ denotes the previous weight of the operator. e'_p is the energy cost saving of every operator

---

Algorithm 2. MALNS Destroy Algorithm

Require: ec_l, λ
Ensure: X
 1: **Init:** Set $X = \{f_{i,j}\}(0 < i < m, 0 < j < n)$
 2:      Set L to palce the emigrated VMs
 3:      $w_p = \frac{1}{z}$, $u_p = \frac{u}{z}$
 4: **while** Number of migrations$\leq u$ **do**
 5:    **for** each do_p **do**
 6:       Get its w_p and u_p
 7:       Destroy the mapping between r_j and s_i according to do_p.
 8:       Add the emigrated r_j to set L
 9:       Denote the saved energy cost of do_p as e'_p
10:    **end for**
11:    Calculate the new daily energy cost nec
12:    **if** $nec < ec_l$ **then**
13:       $ec_l = nec$
14:       Update w_p with (13) to (15)
15:    **else**
16:         **break**
17:    **end if**
18: **end while**
19: Repair the mapping between VM and new server with **Algorithm 3**.

---

after pre-migration. $\tilde{e}$ denotes the largest e'_p. The updated temporary weight of ordinary operator is:

$$w_t = (1 - \tilde{w}) \cdot \frac{e'_p}{\sum_{i=1}^{z} e'_p} \tag{14}$$

where w_t is the updated temporary weight of an ordinary operator. The updated weights, w_n, of each destroy operator is:

$$w_n = \lambda w_p + (1 - \lambda)w \quad (0 \leqslant \lambda \leqslant 1, w \in \{\tilde{w}_t, w_t\}) \tag{15}$$

where w_p is the previous weight of do_p and λ is tradeoff coefficient between basic and temporary weights.

Algorithm 3 shows the process of deploying the emigrated VMs to DC again. Lines 3–10 select target servers with different repair operators. The resulting mapping set X is generated in Lines 11–13.

5   Experiment

5.1   Experimental Setup

We used six simulation datasets, each consists of 100 types of servers and a large batch of user requests over a period of time. The configuration information is shown in **Table 2**.

Algorithm 3. MALNS Repair Algorithm

Require: L

1: **Init** Set X, $\hat{e}c_0 = infinity$
2: **for** each ro_q **do**
3:     **for** each $r_j \in L$ **do**
4:         Select the active server s_i
5:         Migrate r_j to server s_i with operator ro_q
6:         **if** there isn't active server in L **then**
7:             Turn on server s_i according to its energy cost
8:             Migrate r_j to server s_i with operator ro_q
9:         **end if**
10:     **end for**
11:     Calculate the new daily energy cost $\hat{e}c_q$.
12:     **if** $\hat{e}c_q < \hat{e}c_{q-1}$ **then**
13:         Update the mapping set $X = \tilde{f}_{i,j}$
14:     **end if**
15: **end for**
16: **return** X

Table 2. Information of datasets

DataSet	Server type	Requests number	Time (days)
D1	100	137,257	800
D2	100	150,274	1,000
D3	100	160,426	800
D4	100	170,373	1,000
D5	100	176,061	800
D6	100	185,766	1,000

5.2 Comparison Algorithms

We consider PABFD [9], MCC [10], FSS [11] and IGGA [16] as baselines, the details are as follow:

- **PABFD (Power Aware Best Fit Decreasing):** A heuristics algorithm that aims at reducing energy cost by allocating VMs to host that provides the least increase of power consumption.
- **MCC (Minimum Correlation Coefficient):** It identified the correlation coefficient between chosen VM and target host based on the utilization of CPU alone.
- **IGGA (Improved Grouping Genetic Algorithm):** It identified a greedy heuristic algorithm and a swap operation based on genetic algorithm.
- **FSS (Fuzzy Soft Sot):** It identified the correlation coefficient between chosen VM and target host based on a variety of indicators, such as memory, CPU, ratio of memory to CPU, and product of memory and CPU.

52 Y. Lv et al.

5.3 Results and Discussion

We compare the proposed algorithm with the PABFD, MCC, IGGA and FSS. Several metrics for each algorithm are discussed, such as energy cost, total cost, daily resource utilisation and average resource utilisation.

Daily Resource Utilization. Fig. 3(a) and (b) compare the daily CPU and memory utilization for UDA-MALNS and PABFD based on datasets D1. Figure 3(c) and (d) show the situation of UDA-MALNS and MCC based on dataset D2. As shown in Fig 3, the proposed algorithm UDA-MALNS ensures that both CPU and memory can be fully utilized during the period of DC operation and both utilization rates are higher than the other towalgorithm. Figure 3(a) and (b) show PABFD and MCC can't take full advantage of both resources at the same time.

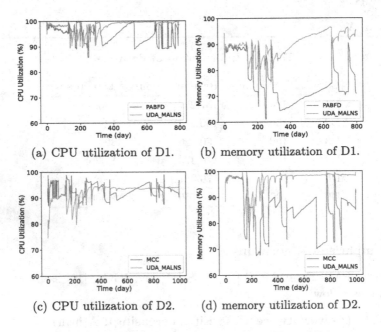

(a) CPU utilization of D1.   (b) memory utilization of D1.

(c) CPU utilization of D2.   (d) memory utilization of D2.

Fig. 3. The load variation of the DC in D1 and D2

Figure 4 shows the comparison of daily CPU and memory utilization with UDA-MALNS and IGGA in datasets D3 and D4. Both algorithms allow the CPU and memory to be kept at a high level of utilisation, but the UDA-MALNS algorithm is has a superior performance than IGGA.

Figure 5 shows the comparison of daily CPU and memory utilisation of UDA-MALNS and FSS in dataset D5 and D6. There are multiple bursts of user demand in in both datasets, it can be seen that the FSS algorithm is less robust than the UDA-MALNS in the face of a surge in user demand.

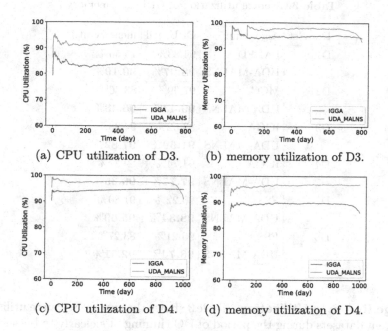

(a) CPU utilization of D3.   (b) memory utilization of D3.

(c) CPU utilization of D4.   (d) memory utilization of D4.

Fig. 4. The load variation of the DC in D3 and D4

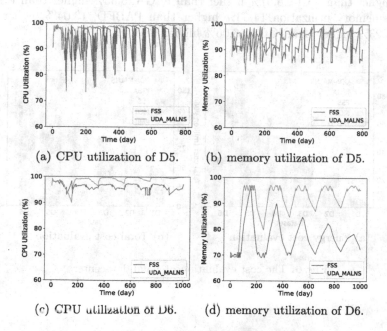

(a) CPU utilization of D5.   (b) memory utilization of D5.

(c) CPU utilization of D6.   (d) memory utilization of D6.

Fig. 5. The load variation of the DC in D5 and D6

Table 3. Average utilization of CPU and memory

DataSet	Algorithm	CPU util	memory util
D1	PABFD	94.83%	75.56%
	UDA-MALNS	**98.07%**	**90.19%**
D2	MCC	97.39%	83.36%
	UDA-MALNS	**99.43%**	**96.43%**
D3	IGGA	83.52%	94.33%
	UDA-MALNS	**91.69%**	**97.82%**
D4	IGGA	94.74%	89.37%
	UDA-MALNS	**97.77%**	**96.35%**
D5	FSS	90.22%	91.80%
	UDA-MALNS	**98.34%**	**95.69%**
D6	FSS	96.21%	83.27%
	UDA-MALNS	**98.74%**	**92.51%**

Average Resource Utilization. Table 3 shows the average resource utilisation in different datasets during the period of DC running, it's clearly to be seen that our approach use the resources in a balance way and achieve higher utilization than other methods. (on average CPU utilization 3.2% higher than PABFD, 2.04% higher than MCC, 5.57% higher than IGGA, 5.33% higher than FSS; on average memory utilization 14.63% higher than PABFD, 13.04% higher than MCC, 5.23% higher than IGGA, 6.06% higher than FSS.

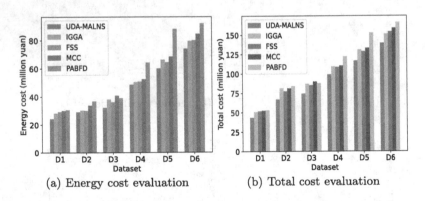

(a) Energy cost evaluation   (b) Total cost evaluation

Fig. 6. The cost evaluation of cloud datacenter

Energy Cost and Total Cost. Figure 6(a) and (b) show the comparison of energy cost and total cost of the proposed algorithm and baselines at different datasets respectively. It can be seen that our proposed UDA-MALNS algorithm outperforms the other algorithms. In this comparison, our method achieves the lowest energy cost among all baselines (on average 23.33% lower than PABFD, 15.69% lower than MCC, 13.1% lower than IGGA, 12.12% lower than FSS) and lowest total cost(on average 19.02% lower than PABFD, 13.14% lower than MCC, 8.12% lower than IGGA, 7.51% lower than FSS)

6 Conclusion

In this paper, we proposed an approach for cost-efficient cloud data center construction and service consolidation. For properly allocate sufficient cloud resources to users and optimize the total hardware cost, we formulate the decision problem as a Bin Packing problem and proposed an adaptive purchasing strategy. In order to save the energy cost, we develop an heuristic algorithm for service migration and consolidation with improved resource utilisation. Experimental results demonstrate that our method has better performance than it's peers. In the future, we plan to process the user demands with some predictive algorithms (e.g., time series prediction, association rules) and update the strategy for saving cost.

Acknowledgment. This work is supported National Key R&D Program of China with Grant number 2018YFB1403602, Chongqing Technological innovation foundations with Grant numbers cstc2019jscx-msxm0652 and cstc2019jscx-fxyd0385, Chongqing Key RD project with Grant number cstc2018jszx-cyzdX0081, Jiangxi Key RD project with Grant number 20181ACE50029. Sponsored by technological program organized by SGCC (No.52094020000U). Technology Innovation and Application Development Foundation of Chongqing under Grant cstc2020jscx-gksbX0010.

References

1. Weiling, L., Xiaoning, S., Kewen, L., Yunni, X., Feifei, C., Qiang, H.: Maximizing reliability of data-intensive workflow systems with active fault tolerance schemes in cloud. In: 2020 IEEE 13th International Conference on Cloud Computing (CLOUD), pp. 462–469 (2020)
2. Pan, Y., Sun, X., Xia, Y., Zheng, W., Luo, X.: A predictive-trend-aware and critical-path-estimation-based method for workflow scheduling upon cloud services. In: 2020 IEEE International Conference on Services Computing (SCC), pp. 162–169 (2020)
3. Quanwang, W., Zhou, M.C., Zhu, Q., Xia, Y., Wen, J.: Moels: multiobjective evolutionary list scheduling for cloud workflows. IEEE Trans. Autom. Sci. Eng. **17**(1), 166–176 (2020)
4. Pan, Y., et al.: A novel approach to scheduling workflows upon cloud resources with fluctuating performance Mob. Notw. Appl. **25**(2), 690–700 (2020)
5. Zhou, Y., et al.: A novel approach to applications deployment with multiple interdenpendent tasks in a hybrid three-layer vehicular computing environment. In: 2021 IEEE International Conference on Systems, Man, and Cybernetics (SMC), pp. 251–256 (2021)

6. Peng, Q., et al.: Reliability-aware and deadline-constrained mobile service composition over opportunistic networks. IEEE Trans. Autom. Sci. Eng. **18**(3), 1012–1025 (2020)

7. Peng, Q., Wu, C., Xia, U., Ma, Y., Wang, X., Jiang, N.: Dosra: a decentralized approach to online edge task scheduling and resource allocation. IEEE Internet Things J. **9**, 4677–4692 (2021)

8. Monil, M.A.H., Rahman, R.M.: VM consolidation approach based on heuristics, fuzzy logic, and migration control. J. Cloud Comput. **5**(1), 1–18 (2016). https://doi.org/10.1186/s13677-016-0059-7

9. Beloglazov, A., Buyya, R.: Optimal online deterministic algorithms and adaptive heuristics for energy and performance efficient dynamic consolidation of virtual machines in cloud data centers. Concurrency Comput. Pract. Experience **24**(13), 1397–1420 (2012)

10. Xiong, F., Zhou, C.: Virtual machine selection and placement for dynamic consolidation in cloud computing environment. Front. Comp. Sci. **9**(2), 322–330 (2015)

11. Baskaran, N., Eswari, R.: CPU-memory aware VM consolidation for cloud data centers. Scalable Comput. **21**(2), 159–172 (2020)

12. Alsadie, D., Alzahrani, E.J., Sohrabi, N., Tari, Z., Zomaya, A.Y.: DTFA: a dynamic threshold-based fuzzy approach for power-efficient VM consolidation. In: 2018 IEEE 17th International Symposium on Network Computing and Applications (NCA) (2018)

13. Wang, J.V., Ganganath, N., Cheng, C.T., Chi, K.T.: Bio-inspired heuristics for VM consolidation in cloud data centers. IEEE Syst. J. **PP**(99), 1–12 (2019)

14. Li, Z., Xinrong, Yu., Lei, Yu., Guo, S., Chang, V.: Energy-efficient and quality-aware VM consolidation method. Future Gener. Comput. Syst. **102**, 789–809 (2020)

15. Farahnakian, F., Pahikkala, T., Liljeberg, P., Plosila, J., Hieu, N.T., Tenhunen, H.: Energy-aware VM consolidation in cloud data centers using utilization prediction model. IEEE Trans. Cloud Comput. **PP**, 1 (2016)

16. Wu, Q., Ishikawa, F., Zhu, Q., Xia, Y.: Energy and migration cost-aware dynamic virtual machine consolidation in heterogeneous cloud datacenters. IEEE Trans. Serv. Comput. **PP**, 1 (1939)

17. Khan, M.A.: An efficient energy-aware approach for dynamic VM consolidation on cloud platforms. Cluster Comput. **24**(4), 3293–3310 (2021). https://doi.org/10.1007/s10586-021-03341-0

18. Xiao, X., et al.: A novel coalitional game-theoretic approach for energy-aware dynamic VM consolidation in heterogeneous cloud datacenters. In: Miller, J., Stroulia, E., Lee, K., Zhang, L.-J. (eds.) ICWS 2019. LNCS, vol. 11512, pp. 95–109. Springer, Cham (2019). https://doi.org/10.1007/978-3-030-23499-7_7

19. Wu, W., Wang, W., Fang, X., Junzhou, L., Vasilakos, A.V.: Electricity price-aware consolidation algorithms for time-sensitive VM services in cloud systems. IEEE Trans. Serv. Comput. **PP**(99), 1 (2019)

20. Mapetu, J., Kong, L., Chen, Z.: A dynamic VM consolidation approach based on load balancing using pearson correlation in cloud computing. J. Supercomputing **77**(6), 5840–5881 (2021)

21. Mandhi, T., Mezni, H.: A prediction-based VM consolidation approach in IaaS cloud data centers. J. Syst. Softw. **146**, 263–285 (2018)

22. Haghshenas, K., Mohammadi, S.: Prediction-based underutilized and destination host selection approaches for energy-efficient dynamic VM consolidation in data centers. J. Supercomputing **76**(12), 10240–10257 (2020). https://doi.org/10.1007/s11227-020-03248-4

23. Lianpeng, L.I., Dong, J., Zuo, D., Zhao, Y., Tianyang, L.I.: Sla-aware and energy-efficient VM consolidation in cloud data centers using host state binary decision tree prediction model. IEICE Trans. Inf. Syst. **E102.D**(10), 1942–1951 (2019)
24. Hu, K., Lin, W., Huang, T., Li, K., Ma, L.: Virtual machine consolidation for NUMA systems: a hybrid heuristic grey wolf approach. In: 2020 IEEE 26th International Conference on Parallel and Distributed Systems (ICPADS) (2020)
25. Wang, S., Zhou, A., Bao, R., Chou, W., Yau, S.S.: Towards green service composition approach in the cloud. IEEE Trans. Serv. Comput. **14**(4), 1238–1250 (2021)
26. Martello, S., Toth, P.: Bin-packing problem. Knapsack Problems: Algorithms and Computer Implementations, pp. 221–245 (1990)
27. Martello, S., Pisinger, D., Vigo, D.: The three-dimensional bin packing problem. Oper. Res. **48**(2), 256–267 (2000)

TSFed: A Two-Stage Federated Learning Framework via Cloud-Edge Collaboration for Services QoS Prediction

Jian Lin, Yusen Li, Zhuo Xu, Weiwei She, and Jianlong Xu[✉]

Shantou University, Shantou 515063, China
{20jlin3,18ysli4,20zxu3,17wwshe,xujianlong}@stu.edu.cn

Abstract. Federated learning-based quality of service (QoS) prediction methods are regularly used to protect user privacy in smart cities. However, federated learning (FL) is fragile for heterogeneous QoS data, and these FL methods usually update a single global model by aggregating diverging gradients, which cannot effectively capture the heterogeneous data features of different users, resulting in less than optimal model convergence speed. Moreover, the existing FL methods do not pay attention to the positive effect of regional similarity of QoS data on model convergence. To address these issues, we propose a two-stage federated learning QoS prediction framework (TSFed) based on cloud-edge collaboration. In the first stage, the cloud server coordinates the user to train a partially optimized pre-training model. In the second stage, the edge server coordinates users to fine-tune the pre-training model. Experiments on real-world datasets show that TSFed can achieve a 21.54%–46.73% reduction in the number of communication rounds and a 29.83%–50.73% reduction in communication delay required to achieve the target prediction accuracy compared to existing approaches.

Keywords: Federated learning · QoS prediction · Cloud-edge collaboration · Smart city

1 Instruction

In recent years, smart city is gradually becoming a reality due to the development of Internet, mobile technology and the sixth generation mobile network (6G) [1,2]. In smart city, various mobile devices and related Internet services (e.g., traffic flow prediction services, point-of-interest (POI) recommendation services, etc.) are gradually being accepted by citizens. Mobile users can handle their daily tasks through recommended Internet services that meet their requirements [3]. It is important to know which services have better QoS values in order to make better service recommendations. A common practice to address this challenge is to collect historical QoS values from users to predict unknown QoS values [4,5]. Classical QoS prediction methods include neighbor-based [6] and model-based [7] collaborative filtering. However, with the formulation of privacy-related

Y. Zhang and L.-J. Zhang (Eds.): ICWS 2022, LNCS 13736, pp. 58–72, 2022.
https://doi.org/10.1007/978-3-031-23579-5_5

laws and regulations (e.g., GDPR) [8] and the increasing emphasis on personal privacy [9,10] it is difficult for smart city systems to collect user raw data. To protect user privacy without compromising model performance, many scholars have applied the federated learning solution [11]. As a new distributed machine learning scenario, federated learning (FL) allows users to collaboratively train a high-quality global model through gradients sharing without exposing their raw data. Recently, many works have designed advanced FL methods to improve the convergence speed of federated learning [12–14]. Konevcny *et al.* [12] proposed an update of structuring and sketching to reduce the time required to complete a round of communication. McMahan *et al.* [14] proposed the Federated Average algorithm (FedAvg), which aims to reduce the number of required communication rounds by increasing the amount of local computation on the user devices and averaging the model weights from the user devices.

However, existing approaches usually update a single global model by directly aggregating model gradients, which cannot effectively capture the heterogeneous QoS data features of different users and may not achieve a satisfactory convergence speed. This is mainly due to the fact that the QoS data distribution of individual users does not represent the overall data distribution and the model gradients obtained by training on heterogeneous data may vary significantly. In addition, existing methods also ignore the positive role of regional similarity of QoS data in model convergence. If users are divided into multiple groups based on geographic regions and the model gradients of users in different groups are aggregated by multiple gradient aggregation centers, not only the heterogeneous QoS data features of different users can be captured, but also users located in the same region with similar data distributions can share a global model.

In this work, we propose a two-stage FL framework for QoS prediction via a cloud-edge collaborative scheme (TSFed) to accelerate the convergence speed of FL-based QoS prediction models. In our proposed framework, there exists one cloud server and multiple edge servers. In the first stage of FL, the cloud server coordinates all users to train a pre-training model that does not need to be fully optimized to provide an initialized model with good generalization capability to the edge servers. In the second stage of FL, each edge server coordinates the user devices in the coverage area to fine-tune the pre-training model with the aim of sharing a global model among users with similar data distribution. Our main contributions are summarized as follows:

- We propose a two-stage federated learning framework for services QoS prediction via a cloud-edge collaboration scheme (TSFed), which not only captures the heterogeneous QoS data features of different users, but also users with similar data distribution can share a global model, effectively improving the convergence of the FL-based QoS prediction model.
- We design a pre-training model training method based on federated learning that does not need to be fully optimized to provide an initialized model with good generalization capability to the edge server.
- We propose a FL-based fine-tuning approach to fine-tune the proposed pre-training model by coordinating users within a region, with the aim of exploit-

ing the regional similarity of QoS data and enabling users with similar data distribution to share a global model.
- We conduct extensive experiments on real datasets to verify the effectiveness of our proposed framework.

2 Related Work

Recently, many scholars have proposed many privacy-preserving approaches based on QoS prediction [15–18]. Zhang et al. [15] proposed a differential privacy-based QoS prediction method, which allows users to obfuscate QoS data by adding Laplacian noise on the raw data, and then adopting conventional neighborhood-based collaborative filtering method for QoS prediction. Badsha et al. [16] proposed a QoS prediction method based on homomorphic encryption, which allows users to homomorphically encrypt their own location and QoS data, and then use collaborative filtering on the homomorphically encrypted data for prediction. However, differential privacy-based approaches greatly reduce the availability of data, and the computational process of homomorphic encryption is very resource-intensive.

Federated learning [14], as an emerging distributed machine learning framework, allows user devices to collaboratively train a global model by sharing model gradients instead of sharing raw data from user device, which helps to protect user privacy and reduce communication costs. Since user devices usually have unstable and expensive connections, the training completion time in the federated learning is largely limited by the communication rounds. McMahan et al. [14] proposed a federated averaging method (FedAvg), which reduces the number of user communications with the central server by increasing the local training epoch. However, some user equipments may be affected by an unstable network state or their own computing resources are limited, so that they cannot complete a pre-negotiated local epochs within a specified time. Therefore, the stability of FedAvg is not satisfactory [19]. Li et al. [19] proposed FedProx, which adds a proximal term based on FedAvg, so that the model after each local update should not be too far away from the global model, thus increasing the stability of federated learning. FedDane [20] applied the idea of approximate Newtonian method on the basis of FedProx to ensure that the model can converge in both convex and non-convex problems. However, the above optimization methods are generally applied to image recognition and language modeling tasks, and few works apply federated learning to QoS prediction tasks. Recently, Zhang et al. [21] proposed a based-QoS federated matrix factorization scheme. Xu et al. [22] proposed the FNCF method, which integrates federated learning into a neural collaborative filtering model.

3 Proposed Framework

In this section, we describe our proposed two-stage federated learning framework via cloud-edge collaboration scheme for services QoS prediction (TSFed) in detail. Specifically, we first present an overview of our framework. All the technical details are described in the following sections, including exploring a pre-training model training method based on FL and a fine-tuning method based on FL.

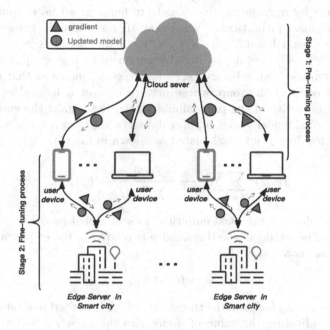

Fig. 1. Overview of TSFed framework.

3.1 Framework Overview

To effectively capture the heterogeneous QoS data features of different users, and enable users with similar data distribution to share a global model, we propose a two-stage federated learning framework via cloud-edge collaboration scheme for QoS prediction (TSFed). Unlike the "server-client" architecture consisting of cloud server and user in a conventional federated learning setup, our proposed framework is a "cloud-edge-client" architecture consisting of three roles, i.e., cloud server, edge servers, and users, as shown in Fig. 1. In the first stage of FL, the cloud server acts as a single model aggregation center to learn a pre-training model by aggregating the model gradients of all users from different geographic regions until the empirical loss of the pre-training model over the all user datasets is less than a specified threshold. In the second stage of FL, each edge server separately coordinates the users in its coverage area to learn an edge global model. The edge server first initializes the edge global model with the pre-training model. Then, it fine-tunes the edge global model by aggregating the model gradients of the users in its coverage area. We present the technical details of the two mentioned components in the following two subsections.

3.2 Pre-training

To provide an initialized model with good generalization capability to edge servers, we propose a new pre-training model training method based on FL. The cloud server acts as a single gradient aggregation center to learn a pre-training model by aggregating the model gradients of all users from different geographic regions. In particular, we divide all users into K groups based on geographic regions, labeled $G_1, \cdots, G_K$, with the number of users in each group being m_k ($k \in [1, K]$), and deploy an edge server in each geographic region. All users are numbered with a binary (k, i), and $User_{k,i}$ indicates that the user is the i-th user of the k-th group, whose private dataset is labeled as $D_{k,i}$. The optimization objective of the pre-training model is to make the empirical loss $f(w)$ of the global model w over all user datasets less than a specified threshold ρ. The empirical loss $f(w)$ is calculated as shown in Eq. (1).

$$f(w) = \sum_{k=1}^{K} \sum_{i=1}^{m_k} \frac{|D_{k,i}|}{\sum_{k=1}^{K} \sum_{i=1}^{m_k} |D_{k,i}|} F_{k,i}(w), \tag{1}$$

where $F_{k,i}(w)$ denotes the local empirical loss of global model w on the local dataset $D_{k,i}$. The setting of the threshold ρ is related to the empirical loss $f(w)$ for round 0, as shown in Eq. (2).

$$\rho = f(w_0) * d, \tag{2}$$

where d is the scaling factor of the threshold, which is limited to a range between 0 and 1. By adjusting the value of d, we can decide when to terminate the pre-training process. The larger the scale factor d, the faster the pre-training terminates; conversely, the slower.

In round t, $User_{k,i}$ first calculates the local empirical loss $F_{k,i}(w_t)$ of the global model w_t on the local dataset as shown in Eq. (3).

$$F_{k,i}(w_t) = \frac{\sum_{j=1}^{|D_{k,i}|} \ell_{((k,i),j)}(w_t)}{|D_{k,i}|}, \tag{3}$$

where $\ell_{((k,i),j)}(w_t)$ denotes the loss function of the j-th record of $D_{k,i}$ and $|D_{k,i}|$ denotes the number of records in the dataset $D_{k,i}$. Then the local model $w_t^{k,i}$ is initialized with the global model w_t and the local model $w_t^{k,i}$ is updated with the private dataset $D_{k,i}$ as shown in Eq. (4).

$$w_t^{k,i} = w - \eta \nabla F_{k,i}(w_t^{k,i}), \tag{4}$$

where η is the learning rate. After multiple local training epochs, the user $User_{k,i}$ sends the local model updates $\nabla F_{k,i}(w_t^{k,i})$ together with the local empirical loss $F_{k,i}(w_t)$ to the cloud server. The cloud server first needs to compute the empirical loss $f(w_t)$, and then decides whether the pre-training process should be terminated by comparing the magnitude of the empirical loss $f(w_t)$ and the threshold ρ.

When $f(w_t)$ is less than the specified threshold ρ, it means that the pre-training process has completed and the cloud server can send the global model w_t to the edge server for model fine-tuning. Notably, the first round of fine-tuning of the pre-training model is designed to be performed on the cloud server, since the local model updates uploaded by the users in round t have not been utilized yet. We replicate the model w_t on the cloud server K times, and denote the replicated model as $w_t^{(cloud,k)}$ ($k \in [1, K]$). Then, the model $w_t^{(cloud,k)}$ is updated by aggregating local model updates for users within the coverage of the k-th edge server, as shown in Eq. (5).

$$w_{t+1}^{(cloud,k)} = w_t^{(cloud,k)} - \sum_{i=1}^{m_k} \frac{|D_{k,i}|}{\sum_{i=1}^{m_k}|D_{k,i}|} \nabla F_{k,i}(w_t^{k,i}), if\ f(w_t) < \rho \qquad (5)$$

After the update is completed, the cloud server sends the updated model $w_{t+1}^{(cloud,k)}$ the corresponding edge servers respectively.

When $f(w_t)$ is greater than the specified threshold ρ, it means that the pre-training process is not completed and the cloud server need to complete the current round of global model updates by aggregating the local model updates of all users, as shown in Eq. (6)

$$w_{t+1} = w_t - \sum_{k=1}^{K}\sum_{i=1}^{m_k} \frac{|D_{k,i}|}{\sum_{k=1}^{K}\sum_{i=1}^{m_k}|D_{k,i}|} \nabla F_{k,i}(w_t^{k,i}), if\ f(w_t) \geq \rho \qquad (6)$$

The cloud server then continues to coordinate all users for training until the empirical loss $f(w_t)$ is less than a specified threshold ρ.

3.3 Fine-Tuning

After the pre-training model is trained, the edge server can fine-tune the pre-training model by coordinating users in its coverage area, with the aim of sharing a global model among users with similar data distribution.

First, we initialize the edge global model $w^{(edge,k)}$ on the edge server using the pre-training model $w^{(cloud,k)}$, as shown in Eq. (7).

$$w^{(edge,k)} = w^{(cloud,k)} \qquad (7)$$

Therefore, the edge server can directly obtains an initialized model with good generalization capability. Then, the edge server fine-tunes the edge global model $w^{(edge,k)}$ by coordinating the users in its coverage area to participate in the training. The optimization objective of fine-tuning is to minimize the empirical loss $f_k(w^{(edge,k)})$ of the model $w^{(edge,k)}$ over all user datasets in its coverage area. The empirical loss $f_k(w^{(edge,k)})$ is calculated as follows.

$$f_k(w^{(edge,k)}) = \sum_{i=1}^{m_k} \frac{|D_{k,i}|}{\sum_{i=1}^{m_k}|D_{k,i}|} F_{k,i}(w^{(edge,k)}) \qquad (8)$$

In round t, user $User_{k,i}$ initializes the local model using the edge global model $w_t^{(edge,k)}$ and then updates the local model with the training dataset $D_{k,i}$. After multiple local training epochs, the user $User_{k,i}$ sends the local model updates $\nabla F_{k,i}(w_t^{k,i})$ to the k-th edge server. The k-th edge server aggregates the local model updates $\nabla F_{k,i}(w_t^{k,i})$ from users in the coverage area and updates the edge global model, as shown in Eq. (9)

$$w_{t+1}^{(edge,k)} = w_t^{(edge,k)} - \sum_{i=1}^{m_k} \frac{|D_{k,i}|}{\sum_{i=1}^{m_k} |D_{k,i}|} \nabla F_{k,i}(w_t^{k,i}) \tag{9}$$

4 Experiment

In this section, we experimentally answer the following research questions.

RQ1. Does our proposed method outperform to state-of-the-art FL-based QoS prediction methods?
RQ2. How does scaling factor d affect model performance?
RQ3. Does increasing the computation on user devices improve model performance?

4.1 Dataset

In our experiments, we utilize the publicly available QoS dataset WS-DREAM [23,24] to evaluate our proposed method. This QoS dataset consists of two sub-datasets, one is the response time dataset (RT) and the other is the throughput dataset (TP). Each sub-dataset collects 1,974,675 records from 339 users distributed in 31 countries invoking 5285 real-world web services distributed in 79 countries. RT refers to the time interval between sending a request and receiving a response. The range of the response time property is 0–20 s. TP refers to the average rate per second of successfully delivering a message size (here in bits) on a communication channel, and the throughput property ranges from 0–1000 kbps.

4.2 Evaluation Metrics

We evaluate the performance of the FL-based QoS prediction model by using the following two metrics.

- **TCR** (Total Communication Rounds). TCR refers to communication rounds required for the model to achieve the target prediction accuracy. It is widely used to measure the convergence speed of FL [14].
- **TCD** (Total Communication Delay). TCD refers to communication delay required for the model to achieve the target prediction accuracy.

Note that we use the mean absolute error (MAE) to measure the prediction accuracy. The formula for calculating the mean absolute error is as follows:

$$MAE = \frac{\sum_{(i,j,R_{ij})\in T} |\hat{R}_{ij} - R_{ij}|}{|T|}, \tag{10}$$

where T denotes the test set, $\hat{R}_{ij}$ is the predicted QoS value of the j-th service invoked by the i-th user, and R_{ij} is the true QoS value of the j-th service invoked by the i-th user.

Since the cloud-edge collaboration-based FL framework adopts a "cloud-edge-client" architecture and involves both cloud-client (or cloud-edge) communication and edge-client communication during the training process, the number of communication rounds in the cloud-edge collaboration-based FL framework includes the number of cloud-client (or cloud-edge) communication rounds and the number of edge-client communication rounds. We use TCR_C, TCR_E to denote the number of cloud-client (or cloud-edge) communication rounds and the number of edge-client communication rounds required to achieve the target prediction accuracy in the cloud-edge collaboration-based FL framework, respectively. We use TCR_{CE} to denote the TCR in the cloud-edge collaboration-based FL framework. TCR_{CE} is calculated as shown below.

$$TCR_{CE} = TCR_C + TCR_E \tag{11}$$

We use experimental results from [25] to calculate TCD. In [25], Xu et al. measure the performance (e.g., communication delay, throughput, etc.) of cloud and edge computing platforms in China, where the communication delay between user device and cloud server communication is 23.6 ms; the communication delay between user device and edge server is 16.1 ms. In addition, we equate the communication latency between the cloud server and the edge server to the latency between the cloud server and the user device. We denote the TCD in the cloud-edge collaboration-based federated learning framework by TCD_{CE}. The formula for TCD_{CE} is as follows.

$$TCD_{CE} = TCR_C \times 23.6 + TCR_E \times 16.1 \tag{12}$$

We denote the TCD in the conventional federated learning framework with "cloud-client" architecture by TCD_{con}. The formula for TCD_{con} is as follows.

$$TCD_{Con} = TCR \times 23.6 \tag{13}$$

4.3 Experimental Setup

User Grouping. Since our proposed FL framework is a "cloud-edge-client" architecture, we need to group all users in the dataset based on geographic regions and deploy an edge server as a central server in each group. In this study, we grouped users based on continents. Due to the small number of users in some continents, we combine geographically close continents into one group, as shown in Fig. 2. Therefore, we set the number of user groups K to 3.

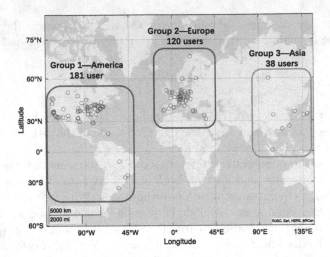

Fig. 2. User Grouping.

Training Set and Test Set. We set the density of the experimental training set to 10%, 15%, 20%, and 25%. As an example, density 25% means that the number of records in the training set is 25% of the original dataset. The training set with density 25% is selected in two steps. (1) 25% of data records are randomly selected from the original dataset; (2) the records are grouped by user and used as a local training set for the user. The remaining 75% of the data records are also grouped by user and used as a local test set for the user, which will be used to evaluate the performance of the model.

Parameter Setup. Our experiments use the conventional matrix factorization model [24] as the local QoS prediction model. For the matrix factorization model, we set the latent feature dimension to 10, the regularization parameters to 0.1, and the optimization function to stochastic gradient descent (SGD) [26] with a learning rate of 0.001 for RT and 0.00003 for TP. For the FL, we set the number of local epochs E_1 for the first stage of FL to 10 and the ratio of users participating in each training round C to 0.1; the number of local epochs E_2 for the second stage of FL to 10 and the ratio of users participating in each training round C to 0.1. In addition, the scaling factor d is set to 26% for RT, 50% for TP.

4.4   Performance Comparison (RQ1)

To evaluate the effectiveness of our proposed framework (TSFed), we first improved federated learning schemes (e.g., FedSGD [14], FedAvg [14], FedProx [19], FedDane [20], and HierFAVG [27]) by integrating these methods with conventional matrix factorization models to make them more suitable for QoS pre-

Table 1. Performance comparison. "$(\cdot)$" indicates the number of communication rounds required when pre-training is complete; "–" indicates that the target prediction accuracy is not reached within the allowed time frame.

QoS	Approach	Density = 10%, MAE = 0.485		Density = 15%, MAE = 0.460		Density = 20%, MAE = 0.440		Density = 25%, MAE = 0.425	
		TCR	TCD(ms)	TCR	TCD(ms)	TCR	TCD(ms)	TCR	TCD(ms)
RT	FedSGD	–	–	–	–	–	–	–	–
	FedAvg	160	3776.0	149	3516.4	200	4720.0	199	4696.4
	FedProx	–	–	149	3516.4	200	4720.0	200	4720.0
	FedDane	–	–	–	–	–	–	–	–
	EFMF	–	–	–	–	–	–	–	–
	HierFAVG	–	–	216	3680.1	–	–	–	–
	TSFed	**116(103)**	**2640.1**	**109(95)**	**2467.4**	**109(90)**	**2429.9**	**106(81)**	**2314.1**
	Improve(%)	27.50%	30.10%	26.85%	29.85%	45.50%	48.54%	46.73%	50.75%
QoS	Approach	Density = 10%, MAE=18.5		Density = 15%, MAE = 17.0		Density = 20%, MAE = 16.5		Density = 25%, MAE = 15.5	
		TCR	TCD(ms)	TCR	TCD(ms)	TCR	TCD(ms)	TCR	TCD(ms)
TP	FedSGD	626	14773.6	536	12649.6	432	10195.2	430	10148.0
	FedAvg	70	1652.0	70	1652.0	66	1557.6	65	1534.0
	FedProx	70	1652.0	70	1652.0	66	1557.6	65	1534.0
	FedDane	–	–	–	–	–	–	–	–
	EFMF	–	–	–	–	–	–	–	–
	HierFAVG	96	1635.6	96	1635.6	104	1771.9	–	–
	TSFed	**53(21)**	**1010.8**	**46(18)**	**875.6**	**45(15)**	**837.0**	**51(14)**	**926.1**
	Improve(%)	24.29%	40.94%	34.29%	48.82%	31.82%	47.90%	21.54%	36.56%

diction application scenarios. Then, we compared our proposed method with the following other methods.

- **FedSGD:** A basic federated learning method that aggregates local gradients;
- **FedAvg:** Based on FedSGD, the number of communication rounds between the user and the central server is reduced by increasing the number of local training epochs for the user;
- **FedProx:** This method improves the stability of federated learning in unstable heterogeneous networks by adding an approximation term to FedAvg. We set the approximation term to 0.1;
- **FedDANE:** This is a federated learning framework that uses Newtonian optimization methods to guarantee model convergence on both convex and non-convex problems.
- **EFMF** [21]: A federated learning-based QoS prediction approach aimed at efficiently reducing computational costs;
- **HierFAVG:** A federated learning framework with a "cloud-edge-client" architecture, which allows multiple edge servers to perform partial model aggregation to reduce communication costs during training. We set the cloud server to aggregate the edge global model after every 7 interactions between the edge server and the user.

At different training set densities, we set the MAE of FedAvg at convergence as the target prediction accuracy. For the RT dataset, the MAE of FedAvg at convergence are 0.485, 0.465, 0.440 and 0.425 for training set densities of 10%, 15%, 20% and 25%, respectively; for the TP dataset, the MAE of FedAvg at convergence are 18.5, 17.0, 16.5 and 15.5 for training set densities of 10%, 15%, 20% and 25%, respectively. In addition, the other parameters are consistent with those described in Sect. 4.3. Table 1 provides the comparative results of the two metrics at different training set densities. As we observed, our proposed TSFed method significantly outperformed the other methods. Specifically, for the RT dataset, TSFed achieves 29.83%–50.73% improvement on TCD and 26.85%–46.73% improvement on TCR at different training set densities. Similarly, for the TP dataset, TSFed achieves 36.56%–48.82% improvement on TCD and 21.54%–34.29% improvement on TCR. Note that all improvements are calculated as the percentage by which TSFed outperforms the other most competitive methods. We also found that although the HierFAVG approach aggregates part of the models with edge servers, it still doesn't perform as well as FedAvg with a "cloud-client" architecture in most cases. In addition, FedSGD fails to converge at the specified time or takes a lot of time to converge, which is due to the fact that FedSGD is only trained locally for one epoch per round. These results show that our proposed method outperforms other methods in the aspect of TCR and TCD.

Table 2. Impact of scaling factor d on TSFed. "$(\cdot)$" indicates the number of communication rounds required to complete the pre-training; "–" indicates that the target prediction accuracy is not reached within the allowed time frame.

QoS	d	MAE = 0.495		MAE = 0.490		MAE = 0.485		MAE = 0.480		MAE = 0.475	
		TCR	TCD(ms)	TCR	TCD(ms)	TCR	TCD(ms)	TCR	TCD(ms)	TCR	TCD(ms)
RT	22%	118(157)	2784.8	141(157)	3327.6	161(157)	3769.6	166(157)	3850.1	176(157)	4011.1
	24%	118(131)	2784.8	133(131)	3123.8	138(131)	3204.3	146(131)	3333.1	159(131)	3542.4
	26%	106(103)	2479.1	110(103)	2543.5	116(103)	2640.1	128(103)	2833.3	161(103)	3364.6
	28%	92(81)	2088.7	98(81)	2185.3	103(81)	2265.8	161(81)	3199.6	–	–
	30%	90(67)	1951.5	102(67)	2144.7	131(67)	2611.6	–	–	–	–

4.5 Impact of Scaling Factor (RQ2)

To evaluate the impact of the scaling factor d on model performance, we increased d from 22% to 30% for RT dataset in steps of 2%. In addition, we set the training set density to 10% and the other parameters are consistent with those described in Sect. 4.3. The evaluation results are provided in Table 2. To visualize the trend of TCD more, we plotted Fig. 3 based on Table 2. From Fig. 3, we can see that TCD shows a trend of decreasing and then increasing with increasing d at each MAE. Taking MAE is set to 0.485 as an example. TCD reaches a minimum when d is 28%, and the TCD at d of 28% is only 60.11% of that at d of 22%. In

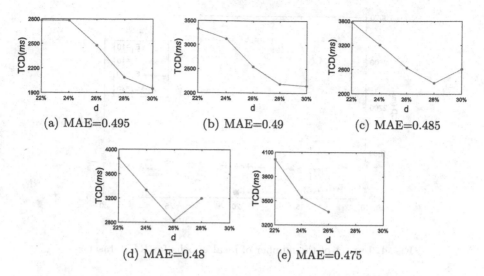

(a) MAE=0.495   (b) MAE=0.49   (c) MAE=0.485

(d) MAE=0.48   (e) MAE=0.475

Fig. 3. Impact of scaling factor d for RT dataset at different target prediction accuracy (MAE is used to indicate the prediction accuracy).

addition, we noticed that the value of d where TCD reaches minimization keeps getting smaller as MAE decreases. Specifically, for the RT dataset, TCD reaches a minimum at d equal to 30%, 28%, 26%, 26%, and 26% when MAE is 0.490, 0.485, 0.480, 0.475, and 0.470. Therefore, when the model is to achieve a lower error, we reduce d appropriately to speed up the convergence of the model and vice versa.

4.6 Impact of the Number of Local Epochs (RQ3)

To evaluate the effect of the number of local epochs, we change the number of local epochs E_1 from 10 to 25 in steps of 5 for the first stage of FL, and change the number of local epochs E_2 from 10 to 30 in steps of 5 for the second stage of FL. For RT dataset, we set the MAE to 0.480 and use it as the target prediction accuracy. In addition, we set the training set density to 10%, and other parameters are consistent with Sect. 4.3. Figure 4 illustrates the evaluation results. When we fix E_2, the TCD generally shows a decreasing trend as E_1 increases. Specifically, for the RT data set, the TCD reaches its lowest point when E_1 is 25. In addition, when we fix E_1, TCD generally shows a decreasing and then increasing trend as E_2 increases, and TCD generally reaches its lowest point when E_2 is 15. Therefore, for RT dataset, the model converges fastest when the number of local epochs in the first stage is 25 and the number of local epochs in the second stage is 15. The above results suggest that we should appropriately increase the local computation in the early stage of model training, and it may be beneficial to attenuate the local computation in the later stage of training.

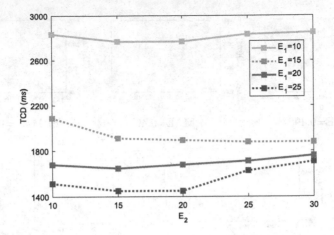

Fig. 4. Impact of the number of local epochs for RT dataset.

5   Conclusion

In this work, we propose a two-stage FL framework for services QoS prediction via a cloud-edge collaboration scheme, which includes a FL-based pre-training process and a FL-based fine-tuning process to accelerate the convergence of FL-based QoS prediction models. Notably, the framework can be combined with traditional QoS prediction models, such as matrix factorization models or neural collaborative filtering models. We argue that traditional FL-based QoS prediction methods usually update a single global model by directly aggregating the model gradients of all users, which cannot effectively capture the heterogeneous QoS data features of different users and cannot effectively exploit the regional similarity of QoS data, resulting in less than optimal model convergence speed and affecting the real-time performance of the model. On the contrary, if users are divided into multiple groups by geographic regions and the model gradients of users within different groups are used to update different global models, the heterogeneous data distribution of different users can be effectively captured and users with similar distribution share the same global model. Therefore, we divide the traditional FL into two stages of training. In the first stage of FL, the cloud server coordinates all user devices to learn a pre-training model. In the second stage of FL, the edge server fine-tunes the pre-training model by coordinating the user devices in the coverage area with the aim of sharing a global model among users with similar data distribution. It should be noted that in the second stage of FL, the central server is deployed to the edge side closer to the user devices, reducing the communication delay between the central server and the user devices for each round. Experimental results based on real-world datasets show that the proposed approach effectively reduces the number of communication rounds and communication delays required for model convergence.

Acknowledgments. This research was financially supported by 2021 Guangdong Province Special Fund for Science and Technology ("major special projects + task list") Project (No. STKJ2021201), Guangdong Province Basic and Applied Basic Research Fund (No. 2021A1515012527), Special projects in key fields of Guangdong universities (No. 2022ZDZX1008) and in part by 2020 Li Ka Shing Foundation Cross-Disciplinary Research Grant (No. 2020LKSFG08D).

References

1. Cirillo, F., Gómez, D., Diez, L., Maestro, I.E., Gilbert, T.B.J., Akhavan, R.: Smart city IoT services creation through large-scale collaboration. IEEE Internet Things J. **7**(6), 5267–5275 (2020)
2. Li, T., Liu, W., Zeng, Z., Xiong, N.N.: DRLR: a deep reinforcement learning based recruitment scheme for massive data collections in 6G-based IoT networks. IEEE Internet Things J. 1–14 (2021)
3. Chen, X., Liang, W., Xu, J., Wang, C., Li, K.-C., Qiu, M.: An efficient service recommendation algorithm for cyber-physical-social systems. IEEE Trans. Netw. Sci. Eng. (2021)
4. Liang, W., Li, Y., Xu, J., Qin, Z., Li, K.C.: QoS prediction and adversarial attack protection for distributed services under DLAAS. IEEE Trans. Comput. pp. 1–14 (2021)
5. Liang, W., et al.: Spatial-temporal aware inductive graph neural network for c-its data recovery. IEEE Trans. Intell. Transp. Syst. (2022)
6. Shao, L., Zhang, J., Wei, Y., Zhao, J., Xie, B., Mei, H.: Personalized QoS prediction for web services via collaborative filtering. In: IEEE International Conference on Web Services (ICWS 2007), pp. 439–446. IEEE (2007)
7. Lo, W., Yin, J., Deng, S., Li, Y., Wu, Z.: An extended matrix factorization approach for QoS prediction in service selection. In: 2012 IEEE Ninth International Conference on Services Computing, pp. 162–169. IEEE (2012)
8. Voigt, P., Von dem Bussche, A.: The EU general data protection regulation (GDPR). A Practical Guide, 1st edn. Springer, Cham, **10**(3152676), 10-5555 (2017). https://doi.org/10.1007/978-3-319-57959-7
9. Zhou, H., Yang, G., Xiang, Y., Bai, Y., Wang, W.: A lightweight matrix factorization for recommendation with local differential privacy in big data. IEEE Trans. Big Data, 1–15 (2021)
10. Wang, C., Wang, S., Cheng, X., He, Y., Xiao, K., Fan, S.: A privacy and efficiency-oriented data sharing mechanism for IoTs. IEEE Trans. Big Data, 1–12 (2022)
11. Khan, L.U., Saad, W., Han, Z., Hossain, E., Hong, C.S.: Federated learning for internet of things: recent advances, taxonomy, and open challenges. IEEE Commun. Surv. Tutor. (2021)
12. Konečnỳ, J., McMahan, H.B., Yu, F.X., Richtárik, P., Suresh, A.T., Bacon, D.: Federated learning: strategies for improving communication efficiency. arXiv preprint arXiv:1610.05492 (2016)
13. Wang, H., Kaplan, Z., Niu, D., Li, B.: Optimizing federated learning on non-iid data with reinforcement learning. In: IEEE INFOCOM 2020-IEEE Conference on Computer Communications, pp. 1698–1707. IEEE (2020)
14. McMahan, B., Moore, E., Ramage, D., Hampson, S., Aguera y Arcas, B.: Communication-efficient learning of deep networks from decentralized data. In: Artificial intelligence and statistics, pp. 1273–1282. PMLR (2017)

15. Zhang, Y., Pan, J., Qi, L., He, Q.: Privacy-preserving quality prediction for edge-based IoT services. Futur. Gener. Comput. Syst. **114**, 336–348 (2021)
16. Badsha, S., et al.: Privacy preserving location-aware personalized web service recommendations. IEEE Trans. Serv. Comput. pp. 1–14 (2018)
17. Badsha, S., Yi, X., Khalil, I., Liu, D., Nepal, S., Lam, K.-Y.: Privacy preserving user based web service recommendations. IEEE Access **6**, 56647–56657 (2018)
18. Gong, B., Xing, T., Liu, Z., Xi, W., Chen, X.: Adaptive client clustering for efficient federated learning over non-iid and imbalanced data. IEEE Trans. Big Data, 1–15 (2022)
19. Li, T., Sahu, A.K., Zaheer, M., Sanjabi, M., Talwalkar, A., Smith, V.: Federated optimization in heterogeneous networks. Proc. Mach. Learn. Syst. **2**, 429–450 (2020)
20. Li, T., Sahu, A.K., Zaheer, M., Sanjabi, M., Talwalkar, A., Smithy, V.: Feddane: a federated newton-type method. In: 2019 53rd Asilomar Conference on Signals, Systems, and Computers, pp. 1227–1231. IEEE (2019)
21. Zhang, Y., Zhang, P., Luo, Y., Luo, J.: Efficient and privacy-preserving federated QoS prediction for cloud services. In: 2020 IEEE International Conference on Web Services (ICWS), pp. 549–553. IEEE (2020)
22. Xu, J., Lin, J., Liang, W., Li, K.-C.: Privacy preserving personalized blockchain reliability prediction via federated learning in IoT environments. Cluster Comput. 1–12 (2021)
23. Zheng, Z., Ma, H., Lyu, M.R., King, I.: Collaborative web service QoS prediction via neighborhood integrated matrix factorization. IEEE Trans. Serv. Comput. **6**(3), 289–299 (2012)
24. Zheng, Z., Zhang, Y., Lyu, M.R.: Investigating QoS of real-world web services. IEEE Trans. Serv. Comput. **7**(1), 32–39 (2012)
25. Xu, M., et al.: From cloud to edge: a first look at public edge platforms. In: Proceedings of the 21st ACM Internet Measurement Conference, pp. 37–53 (2021)
26. Shapiro, A., Wardi, Y.: Convergence analysis of gradient descent stochastic algorithms. J. Optim. Theory Appl. **91**(2), 439–454 (1996)
27. Liu, L., Zhang, J., Song, S.H., Letaief, K.B.: Client-edge-cloud hierarchical federated learning. In: ICC 2020–2020 IEEE International Conference on Communications (ICC), pp. 1–6. IEEE (2020)

Sequential Recommendation Based on Pairs of Interest and Graph Structure

Hao Liu[✉]

Shandong University, Jinan, Shandong 250101, China
lestis@mail.sdu.edu.cn

Abstract. The recommendation system can recommend information to users efficaciously, which helps many users to obtain information in different fields. The chronological order of user-item interactions can reveal time-evolving and sequential user behaviors in many recommender systems. The difficulty of modeling user interests has always been a challenge. The recommendation is a research topic to provide users with personalized items of interest. However, most existing approaches equally treat simple textual information as the input to learn the representation of an item, ignoring the user's interest and structure information of the network. In the recommendation system, users and items and the interaction of their information have a crucial impact on the efficiency and accuracy of the recommendations. However, most recommendation systems are usually designed based only on users. with little consideration given to obtaining other factors that contribute to recommendation behavior. Therefore, we propose a method based on the user's periodic pairs of interest and graph structure to obtain as much effective information as possible to recommend items. Extensive offline experiments on large-scale real data show that our method outperforms the representative baselines.

1 Introduction

In the context of the age of big data, recommender systems(RS), which work for adapting multiple user interests with gigantic property items, are diffusely arranged in all aspects of network applications, incorporating paper recommendation in the academic network, social media, and Commodity recommendations for e-commerce platforms. The ever-increasing number of informational items have been published over the last decades, resulting in a problem known as 'information overload'. This phenomenon is especially serious in network information platforms. Therefore, an effective recommendation system plays a very important role in the Internet information platform.

Many traditional recommendation models, e.g., Collaborative filtering and matrix factorization learn a valid favor prediction function with user-item interplay records. Most accustomed methods are effective, these approaches suffer from a series of issues because of data sparsity. With the express growth of network online technology, certain methods are advanced to include miscellaneous resources and data for enhancing recommendation capability.

Most recommendation systems contain very complex information and different recommendation systems have various advantages and disadvantages. Existing paper recommender systems suffer from a number of limitations. Besides Google Scholar, Microsoft Academic, Semantic Scholar, Web of Science, and a handful of other players, the vast majority of paper search engines are restricted to particular research domains such as the PubMed database for medicine and biology, and IEEE Xplore for Engineering disciplines. Many paper recommendation systems are very limited. Besides Web of Science, Microsoft Academic, Google Scholar, and a few others, the many search engines are limited to particular research domains. Also, some proposed user recommender systems employ collaborative filtering for generating user recommendations [21].

In recommender systems(RS), a large amount of information is often needed to perform the work of completing the information related to the user. Knowledge graphs(KG) have a good role in supplementing information, have been utilized from they can involve wide information in the form of machine-readable entity-relation-entity triplets, which are very useful in recommender systems.

The recent development of GNN can be categorized into spectral and non-spectral approaches. Spectral approaches employ the tools in signal processing and transform the convolutional operation in the graph domain to much simpler operations of the Laplacian spectrum [27]. Non-spectral methods expound convolutions diametrically on the graph within spatially close nodes. Graph attention network provides a promising framework by combining graph neural networks with attention mechanisms in handling graphs with arbitrary structures [28].

Most model uses a graph convolutional network (GCN) [12], which is incorporated in a GNN to generate high-order item connectivity features. However, in these models, items look identical to all users [24, 30, 35], and using GCN with KGs still has drawbacks such as missing comparisons between entities of different layers. Moreover, such models often fail to capture the interaction between user and item, so we provide a method that can better and more accurately capture the interaction between user and item (Fig. 1).

There are several advantages of using the knowledge graph to make recommendations. 1) The rich semantic associations can help uncover potential connections. 2) The diversity of relationships can help extend user interests to improve recommendation diversity. 3) KG can connect user history recommend the item and provide interpretability. The challenge of applying KG to RS stems from the complex graph structure, multiple types of entities, and relationships in KG. Previous work learns the representation of entities and relationships by KG embedding; or designing meta-paths to aggregate neighbor information. Recent work uses GNN to capture item-item relationships or user-item relationships. Such an approach is very beneficial for working with recommender systems. Our approach also adopts this strategy.

Recently, many approaches have been advanced to develop diverse auxiliary information. For paper recommendations, two types of auxiliary information are widely adopted for better recommendations, including structural and textual information. The former type refers to paper citation relationships, i.e., papers

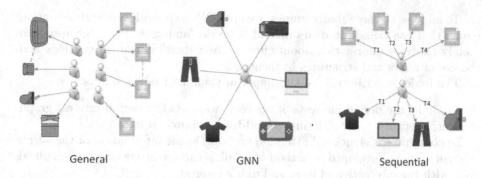

General   GNN   Sequential

Fig. 1. Network Architecture in Recommender Systems. The academic network includes author nodes, paper nodes, and conference nodes. The E-Commodity Network contains information about user nodes and product(item) nodes. Each node in these networks contains different information and there are many interactions between the nodes.

that a paper cites or that cite it [1]. The structure of paper citations may indicate the influence of one paper on another, but it ignores the real content and semantics of the paper. [12] points out another issue that some newly published papers may not be cited and some researchers prefer to cite their own less relevant papers. The paper that the author will interconnect with may rely on the papers visited in the past. But, the notable addition of authors or papers makes sequential recommender systems still confront the challenge that the hardness of modeling the period author interests.

In the product recommendation system, for the user or customers, as e-commerce continues to grow in size and the number and variety of products grows rapidly, it takes a lot of time for customers to find the products they want to buy. The challenge in this type of recommendation is how we can capture effective interaction information. sequential recommendation captures the serialized patterns in the item sequence and recommends the next item of interest for the user. There is mainly Markov chain (MC) based, RNN based, attention-based, and self-attention mechanism-based approaches [5]. With the advent of GNNs, some works convert item sequences into graph structures and capture the transfer patterns in them with GNNs. The sequential order of user-item interrelations can disclose time-evolving and chronological author behaviors.

Most of the gnn methods mentioned above are only computed mainly based on the content of the nodes. However, in social networks, a community or pathway is oftentimes composed of nodes that are densely interconnected with each other but several hops away. Therefore, the structure of the graph is also very important.

To address all these shortcomings, we use GNN to provide a recommendation model that can be adjusted to different scenarios and networks. This approach mainly captures information about effective user-item interest interactions and the use of nodes and structures in the graph.

The major contributions of this paper are summarized as follows:

- To model the period interests of the user, we provide a period interest graph neural network to catch items' period-term contextual information.
- To compute the structural attention and obtain the information of the graph structure, we developed a method of graph structure attention and combined it with the interaction of item and user's interest.
- Extensive offline experiments on large-scale real data show that our method outperforms the representative baselines.

2   Related Work

The first type of paper recommendation is based on the citation structure, i.e., the papers it cites and those citing it. The constructed paper graph is further mined to calculate paper similarity and generate paper recommendations. For example, [1] construct paper representation based on TF-IDF technology, which is heavily relied on the term frequency. The similarity between papers based on citation references is used as weights to build user and paper profiles. However, not all relevant works can be fully covered in one paper. To alleviate this issue, [2] further improve their previous model by extending a paper's reference list with the involvement of the top-N relevant papers. Moreover, [3] build a basic paper graph based on the reference citations. A random walk algorithm is devised to generate recommendation items. To sum up, the underlying assumption of this research line stresses that the citation topology can accurately reflect paper relatedness. However, in many cases, such an assumption cannot hold because: (1) most recently published papers cannot be referred to by previous papers; (2) some valuable references may be missing due to the unawareness of researchers; and (3) some irrelevant or less relevant papers may be adopted in the reference list, for example, some other papers from the same authors.

Insight of the achievement of KGs in an extensive assortment of works, researchers have developed KG-aware recommendation models, many of which have benefited from graph neural networks (GNN) which capture high-order structures in graphs and refine the embeddings of users and items. Most of the information in a recommender system has a graph structure, such as social relationships, knowledge graphs, bipartite graphs composed of user-item interactions, and item transfer graphs in sequences. GNN is able to capture higher-order interactions through iterative propagation and can effectively integrate side information (auxiliary information) such as social relationships and knowledge graphs.

The different types of recommendation systems differ in many things. In academic networks, new researchers, have to spend more time searching for articles they are interested in. Therefore, the paper recommendation is more important than before. Many paper (RS)s are very restricted. With the exception of Web of Science, Microsoft Academic, Google Scholar, and a few other search engines, many are limited to specific areas of research. Also, some proposed user recommender systems employ collaborative filtering for generating user recommendations [21]. In order to mitigate this problem, many academic search engines have begun to add recommendation systems [17,18]. Collaborative filtering (CF) has been widely adopted in recommendation systems, but CF often generates poor performance since the user-item interaction matrix is very sparse in many fields. So, the auxiliary information is introduced to enhance recommendation performance.

Guibing and Bowei propose a two-level attentive neural network called TAAS to capture the semantic correlation between title and abstract for paper ranking and recommendation [22]. To settle the challenges in the intent recommendation, Fan and Shaohua method interactions in intent recommendation system with a Heterogeneous Information Network(HIN) and provide a novel metapath-guided GNN model for intent ranking and suggestion, called MEIRec [15].

3   Method

For different scenarios, whether it is recommending items to relevant authors in academic networks or recommending products(items) to users in e-commerce networks, these can be considered as networks or graphs, and we can treat them as a series of processing operations in the knowledge graph.

A user's interest describes the user's present preference and is dependent on some lately accessed items in a period. The items user will interact with in the near future are likely to be related to the items she just interacted with(visited). Therefore, it is very important in the sequential recommendation to efficaciously method the user's interest, as incarnated by recently accessed items.

First, we must explicitly model the user's interest, our method conduct a sliding window strategy to split the item sequence into fine-grained subsequences. For each user u, we extract every $|L|$ successive items as input L_u $l = (I_l, I_{l+1}, \ldots, I_{l+|L|-1})$ is the l-th sub-sequence of user u. GNNs has their ability to structure learning, so it's a good match for the task of aggregating the items in L_u,l to learn user interests (Fig. 3).

Then, we demand to set up a graph to seize the connections between items because item sequences are not inherently graphs for GNN training. We extract several subsequent items (two items in our experiments) and add edges between them.

We do this for each user and count the number of edges of extracted item pairs across all users. After this performance, we row-normalize the adjacency matrix. After the above process, we can extract relevant items that appear closer to one another in the sequence. As the Fig. 2 shows, we designate the extracted

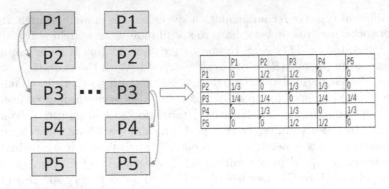

	P1	P2	P3	P4	P5
P1	0	1/2	1/2	0	0
P2	1/3	0	1/3	1/3	0
P3	1/4	1/4	0	1/4	1/4
P4	0	1/3	1/3	0	1/3
P5	0	0	1/2	1/2	0

Fig. 2. Item adjacent matrix construction example. We have taken the academic network as an example, P1, P2.... ... P5 represents the paper nodes (nodes contain relevant information, such as keywords, abstracts, etc.), the information of the nodes in this network structure is richer, that is, the importance of the nodes is greater than the importance of the structure, so we reduce the range of walking between the nodes, focus on getting the information of the nodes (relevant information of the paper, etc.), so that we can capture the information of the (user-item) pairs effectively.

adjacency matrix as A, A_i and k express the normalized node weight of item k regarding item i. And the neighboring items of item i is denoted as N_i.

We next use a GNN to aggregate the neighboring items in L_u, L_l for learning the user's interest representation. For an item j in the l-th short-term window L_u, L_l, its input embedding is represented as $e_j \in R^d$. So we can acquire user interest:

$$\mathbf{h}_i = \tanh\left(\mathbf{W}^{(1)} \cdot \left[\sum_{k \in \mathcal{N}_i} e_k A_{i,k}; e_i\right]\right), \forall i \in L_{u,l} \tag{1}$$

$$\mathbf{p}_{u,l}^S = \tanh\left(\mathbf{W}^{(2)} \cdot \left[\frac{1}{|L|}\sum_{i \in L_{u,l}} \mathbf{h}_i; \mathbf{p}_u\right]\right) \tag{2}$$

S denotes that the representation is from the user interest and $W^{(1)}$ and $W^{(2)}$ are the parameters. ; represent vertical concatenation, $p_{u,l}^S$ denotes which items are closely relevant to the items in $L_{u,l}$ by aggregating neighbors of items in $L_{u,l}$. So, we can acquire the user will access the next item by summarizing the user's term interest.

$$\mathbf{p}_{u',l}^S = \tanh\left(\mathbf{W}^{(3)} \cdot \left[\frac{1}{|2L|}\sum_{i \in L_{u',l}} \mathbf{h}_{i+1}; \mathbf{p}_{u'}\right]\right) \tag{3}$$

With the adjustment of the $W^{(3)}$ parameter, we can control the range of interactions between items, depending mainly on whether the important points of interest are information about the nodes or about the structure.

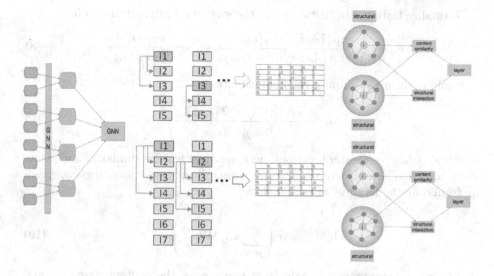

Fig. 3. The frame of our model.

For each graph entered, each node with its features and structural fingerprints. In content, features of the two nodes will be used to compute their content similarity; In structure, structural fingerprints of the two nodes will be used to evaluate their interaction.

Specifically, given a graph of n nodes G = (V,E) , V represent set of the nodes, and E represent set of the edges; then we need to evaluate the content similarity and structural interaction between nodes, for example:

$$e_{ij} = \mathcal{A}_{fea}\left(\mathbf{Wh}_i, \mathbf{Wh}_j\right) \tag{4}$$

$$s_{ij} = \mathcal{A}_{str}\left(F_i, F_j\right) \tag{5}$$

$$\mathcal{A}_{fea}\left(\mathbf{Wh}_i, \mathbf{Wh}_j\right) = \mathbf{a}^{\top}\left(\mathbf{Wh}_i \| \mathbf{Wh}_j\right) \tag{6}$$

$\mathcal{A}_{fea}$ to acquire similarity between the feature of h_i and h_j, $\mathcal{A}_{str}\left(F_i, F_j\right)$ quantifies the interaction between two fingerprints W denotes the transformation that maps the node features to a latent space. Next, w_i and w_i denotes weights of the fingerprints for node i and j, then we can evaluate the structural interactions by Jacard similarity:

$$\mathcal{A}_{str}\left(F_i, F_j\right) = \frac{\sum_{p\in(V_i\cup V_j)}\min\left(w_{ip}, w_{jp}\right)}{\sum_{p\in(V_i\cup V_j)}\max\left(w_{ip}, w_{jp}\right)} \tag{7}$$

Normalize feature similarities 4 and the structural interactions as 5

$$\bar{e}_{ij} \leftarrow \frac{\exp\left(\text{LeakyRelu}\left(e_{ij}\right)\right)}{\sum \exp\left(\text{ LeakyRelu }\left(e_{ik}\right)\right)}, \bar{s}_{ij} \leftarrow \frac{\exp\left(s_{ij}\right)}{\sum \exp\left(s_{ik}\right)} \qquad (8)$$

combine them to compute the final attention:

$$a_{ij} = \frac{\alpha\left(\bar{e}_{ij}\right)\bar{e}_{ij} + \beta\left(\bar{s}_{ij}\right)\bar{s}_{ij}}{\alpha_{(\bar{e}_{ij})} + \beta_{(\bar{s}_{ij})}} \qquad (9)$$

α and β denote transfer functions, we can adjust feature similarity and structure interaction scores before combining them. Then, we perform message passing to update the features of each node as:

$$\mathbf{h}_i^{(t+1)} = \sigma\left(\sum_{j \in \mathcal{N}_i} a_{ij} \mathbf{W} \mathbf{h}_j^{(t)}\right) \qquad (10)$$

our model simultaneously calculates two scores: the content-based e_{ij} and structure-based s_{ij}, and combine them together. By associating the above formulas, we can obtain the results of the user-item pairs of interest and the final expression formula.

4   Experiments

In this section, we introduce the datasets, baseline models, and experiment setup, followed by the results and discussion.

4.1   Datasets

We have conducted extensive experiments on real-world datasets: Item's industrial dataset and Yelp's benchmark dataset. Those dataset included interactions between users and companies and records user information (e.g., id, review count and fans), item information (e.g., id, city and stars) and up to 10 user interactions. We also collected some relevant datasets on books and CDs, and some e-commerce datasets(Items), which were fully used in the experiments.

ACL Anthology Network (AAN) involves papers relevant to Natural Language Processing. The papers belong to disparate venues involving EMNLP, COLING, ACL, and EACL. After excluding several papers with absent information, we possess 21,455 papers, 312 venues, 17,342 authors, and 113367 citation relations. For the labeling job, we accepted a like way as applied to the DBLP.

For each interaction, we randomly sample 5 items that the target user did not engage with before as negative instances. For each user, we hold the latest 30 instances as the test set and utilizes the remaining data for training.

In order to test the capability, we gather real-world data from DBLP and Aminer. Especially, we choose two disparate conference series as the experimental subjects: AI and Datamining. Specifically, we gather the following information: (1) user information, involving the user id name; (2) conference information, involving the conference id and the accepted papers; (3) paper information, involving the paper id, the title, the authors, and the abstract.

Then, in the DBLP, we delete the users who don't possess any tags in these conferences or don't possess publications. Finally, we have a valid dataset.

The dataset citeulike-a is extracted from CiteULike3, and the other dataset PRSDataset comes from CSPubGuru4. For both datasets, we remove the items with missing and defective abstracts as well as their relative interactions. We also filter out the users who have interactions with at most one item. Finally, the citeulike-a dataset is composed of 5548 users, 10987 items (papers), and 134510 user-item pairs. The PRSDataset dataset consists of 2453 users, 21940 items, and 35969 user-item pairs. Basic text processing is adopted to remove stop words from the title and abstract, as well as the segmented (abstract) sentences with less than 20 characters.

Cora is a single graph of 2.7K nodes, TU-IMDB has 1.5K graphs with 13 nodes on average and TU-MUTAG has 188 molecules with 18 nodes. Although small datasets are useful as sanity checks for new ideas, they can become a liability in the long run as new GNN models will be designed to overfit the small test sets instead of searching for more generalizable architectures [24, 25].

Table 1. 10-hop

Method	AAN	DBLP	citeulike-a	Aminer	Cora	CDs	Books	Items
GNN	0.529	0.667	0.566	0.569	0.666	0.424	0.65	0.354
GAT	0.547	0.698	0.506	0.605	0.735	0.525	0.557	0.385
CDL	0.541	0.564	0.669	0.754	0.678	0.522	0.357	0.475
ConvMF	0.447	0.588	0.708	0.775	0.571	0.457	0.47	0.411
LDA-TM	0.672	0.452	0.508	0.688	0.655	0.624	0.454	0.357
MEIRec	0.566	0.604	0.687	0.686	0.704	0.557	0.684	0.675
TAAS	0.758	0.687	0.712	0.674	0.799	0.354	0.387	0.412
Our Method	**0.877**	**0.709**	**0.712**	**0.798**	**0.812**	**0.777**	**0.687**	**0.688**

4.2   Baselines

In this segment, we narrate details about baseline paper recommendation methods and revisions of the offered method used for contrast. We mainly compare our model with the following paper recommendation methods.

CDL [13] attempts to combine an auto-encoder neural model (for better item representation based on textual information) and a traditional collaborative filtering method.

Table 2. AUC evaluation experiment

Method	acdm auc%	Items auc%
GNN	−2.88	−1.65
GAT	1.1	−0.57
CDL	−3.2	−0.37
ConvMF	−1.33	1.87
LDA-TM	−1.2	0.44
MEIRec	3.11	1.64
TAAS	3.27	1.87
Adaptive	3.57	1.98
Our Method	**3.61**	**1.89**

ConvMF [14] applies a convolution neural network to learn the representation of items, and then jointly model user preference by integrating with a traditional matrix factorization model.

LDA-TM [9]. The method utilizes LDA modeling to the detail of papers to produce paper recommendations. In order to produce topics, a Gensim wrapper of LDA topic modeling from MALLET is adopted to the titles and abstracts of research papers. The method produces good results on the informed parameters settings.

MEIRec [15] objects and interactions in intent ranking and recommendation system with a HIN and propose a novel metapath-guided GNN method for the intent recommendation. MEIRec utilizes metapath-guided neighbors to exploit rich structural information.

TAAS [22] can capture the semantic correlation between title and abstract for paper or conference ranking and recommendation.

ATBRG propose a new framework named ATBRG to effectively capture structural relations of target user-item pairs over KG. ATBRG propose the graph connect and graph prune techniques to construct adaptive target-behavior relational graph.

4.3 Results

Firstly, we divide the academic network and commodity (e-commerce) network, and select some sub-network networks with more features and more complex structures, and run different models in these sub-networks or subgraphs to observe their respective effects, as shown in Table 1 (set the range to 10hop), in a lesser range of networks our models are advantageous compared to others (Figs. 4 and 5).

In the next experimental part, we split the model into several parts, naming the part that uses gnn clustering as M_g, the middle part that uses the temporal

Table 3. Results on the datasets

Method	AAN	DBLP	citeulike-a	Aminer	Cora	CDs	Books	Items
GNN	0.38	0.44	0.56	0.35	0.55	0.42	0.51	0.33
	0.59	0.66	0.66	0.59	0.46	0.24	0.65	0.34
GAT	0.42	0.25	0.45	0.24	0.21	0.44	0.46	0.27
	0.547	0.698	0.506	0.605	0.735	0.525	0.557	0.385
CDL	0.55	0.2	0.42	0.15	0.15	0.21	0.52	0.3
	0.541	0.564	0.669	0.754	0.678	0.522	0.357	0.475
ConvMF	0.29	0.53	0.4	0.56	0.44	0.34	0.51	0.5
	0.447	0.588	0.708	0.775	0.571	0.457	0.47	0.411
LDA-TM	0.55	0.59	0.4	0.59	0.5	0.25	0.41	0.17
	0.672	0.452	0.508	0.688	0.655	0.624	0.454	0.357
MEIRec	0.38	0.51	0.24	0.14	0.39	0.23	0.57	0.45
	0.566	0.604	0.687	0.686	0.704	0.557	0.684	0.675
Adapt	0.33	0.33	0.29	0.59	0.39	0.12	0.43	0.31
	0.26	0.24	0.45	0.24	0.59	0.35	0.39	0.39
TAAS	0.58	0.31	0.58	0.34	0.53	0.41	0.53	0.25
	0.758	0.687	0.712	0.674	0.799	0.354	0.387	0.412
Our Method	**0.554**	**0.644**	**0.569**	**0.58**	**0.67**	**0.62**	**0.544**	**0.712**
	0.877	**0.709**	**0.712**	**0.798**	**0.812**	**0.777**	**0.687**	**0.688**

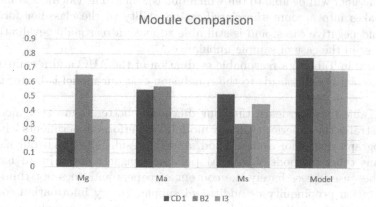

Fig. 4. Module comparison. CD1, B2 and I3 are from different e-commerce datasets, and we use different datasets to conduct comparison experiments on different modules, and the results show that our model is better than the others.

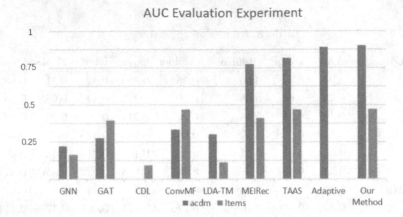

Fig. 5. AUC Evaluation Experiment

adjacency matrix to capture interest as M_a, and the part that combines the graph structure with node information embedding as M_s. Finally, we make a comparison between these split models and the overall model on the commodity network dataset. As shown in Table, from this part of the experimental results table, we can conclude that the overall model results are better than the others.

We have used AUC to reasonably evaluate our model. When using normalized units, the area under the curve (often referred to as simply the AUC) is equal to the probability that a classifier will rank a randomly chosen positive instance higher than a randomly chosen negative one (assuming 'positive' ranks higher than 'negative'). In other words, when given one randomly selected positive instance and one randomly selected negative instance, AUC is the probability that the classifier will be able to tell which one is which. The calculation method of AUC takes into account the classification ability of the classifier for both positive and negative cases, and is still able to make a reasonable evaluation of the classifier in the case of sample imbalance.

As shown in Table 2, a reasonable evaluation of the AUC and a comparison with the chosen baseline leads to the conclusion that our model is better to the others.

From Table 3 we can learn that our method is better than other methods, which illustrates the superiority of our model. We perform experiments with different subgraph ranges for each method, and the results show that our method outperforms other methods. LDA-TM performs unsuccessfully in all baseline methods because it uses barely the content of papers and does not think over papers' citation propinquity or additional supplementary information sources. CDL is a relatively shallow model, and ConvMF applies a convolution neural network (CNN) to learn the representation of papers, the two methods ignore the author's interest and cannot find effective information. The MEIRec places too much emphasis on structural information compared to other methods. TAAS focuses on textual information, the feature of nodes, and does not involve structure. Compared with other methods, our method is better.

5   Conclusion

In this paper, we presented a method that relied on the user's periodic interest and graph network structure to obtain as much effective information as possible to recommend items. We model the period interests of the user and computing the structural attention, our method developed a way of graph structure attention and combined it with the user's interest. Extensive offline experiments on real data show that our method outperforms the representative others.

References

1. Kang, W.-C., McAuley, J.: Self-attentive sequential recommendation. In: 2018 IEEE International Conference on Data Mining (ICDM). IEEE (2018)
2. Chen, X., et al.: Sequential recommendation with user memory networks. In: Proceedings of the Eleventh ACM International Conference on Web Search and Data Mining (2018)
3. Tang, J., Wang, K.: Personalized top-n sequential recommendation via convolutional sequence embedding. In: Proceedings of the Eleventh ACM International Conference on Web Search and Data Mining (2018)
4. Liu, Q., et al.: Context-aware sequential recommendation. In: 2016 IEEE 16th International Conference on Data Mining (ICDM). IEEE (2016)
5. Sun, F., et al.: BERT4Rec: sequential recommendation with bidirectional encoder representations from transformer. In: Proceedings of the 28th ACM International Conference on Information and Knowledge Management (2019)
6. Bansal, T., Belanger, D., McCallum, A.: Ask the GRU: multi-task learning for deep text recommendations, In: Proceedings of the 10th ACM Conference on Recommender Systems, New York, NY, USA, pp. 107–114 (2016)
7. Pazzani, M.J., Billsus, D.: Content-based recommendation systems. In: Brusilovsky, P., Kobsa, A., Nejdl, W. (eds.) The Adaptive Web. LNCS, vol. 4321, pp. 325–341. Springer, Heidelberg (2007). https://doi.org/10.1007/978-3-540-72079-9_10
8. Sugiyama, K., Kan, M.-Y.: Exploiting potential citation papers in scholarly paper recommendation. In: Proceedings of the 13th ACM/IEEE-CS Joint Conference on Digital Libraries (JCDL), pp. 153–162 (2013)
9. Amami, M., Pasi, G., Stella, F., Faiz, R.: An LDA-based approach to scientific paper recommendation. In: Métais, E., Meziane, F., Saraee, M., Sugumaran, V., Vadera, S. (eds.) NLDB 2016. LNCS, vol. 9612, pp. 200–210. Springer, Cham (2016). https://doi.org/10.1007/978-3-319-41754-7_17
10. He, R., McAuley, J.: Fusing similarity models with Markov chains for sparse sequential recommendation. In: 2016 IEEE 16th International Conference on Data Mining (ICDM). IEEE (2016)
11. Bhagavatula, C., Feldman, S., Power, R., Ammar, W.: Content-based citation recommendation. In: Proceedings of the 2018 Conference of the North American Chapter of the Association for Computational Linguistics: Human Language Technologies, Volume 1 (Long Papers), pp. 238–251. Association for Computational Linguistics, New Orleans, Louisiana (2018)
12. Hassan, H.A.M.: Personalized research paper recommendation using deep learning. In: Proceedings of the 25th Conference on User Modeling, Adaptation and Personalization (UMAP), pp. 327–330 (2017)

13. Wang, H., Wang, N., Yeung, D.-Y.: Collaborative deep learning for recommender systems. In: Proceedings of the 21th ACM SIGKDD International Conference on Knowledge Discovery and Data Mining (KDD), pp. 1235–1244 (2015)
14. Kim, D., Park, C., Oh, J., Lee, S., Yu, H.: Convolutional matrix factorization for document context-aware recommendation (recsys). In: Proceedings of the 10th ACM Conference on Recommender Systems, pp. 233–240 (2016)
15. Fan, S., et al.: Metapath-guided heterogeneous graph neural network for intent recommendation. In: Proceedings of the 25th ACM SIGKDD International Conference on Knowledge Discovery Data Mining, pp. 2478–86. Anchorage AK USA. ACM (2019)
16. Dong, Y., Ma, H., Shen, Z., Wang, K.: A century of science: globalization of scientific collaborations, citations, and innovations. In: Proceedings ofthe 23rd ACM SIGKDD International Conference on Knowledge Discovery and Data Mining, pp. 1437–1446 (2017)
17. Bollacker, K.D., Lawrence, S., Giles, C.L.: A system for automatic personalized tracking of scientific literature on the web. In: Proceedings of the Fourth ACM Conference on Digital Libraries, pp. 105–113. ACM (1999)
18. Torres, R., McNee, S.M., Abel, M., Konstan, J.A., Riedl, J.: Enhancing digital libraries with TechLens+. In: Proceedings of the 4th ACM/IEEE-CS Joint conference on Digital Libraries, pp. 228–236. ACM (2004)
19. Beel, J., Aizawa, A., Breitinger, C., Gipp, B.: Mr. DLib: recommendations-as-a-service (RaaS) for academia. In: 2017ACM/IEEE Joint Conference on Digital Libraries (JCDL), pp. 1–2. IEEE (2017)
20. Bhagavatula, C., Feldman, S., Power, R., Ammar, W.: Content-based citation recommendation. In: NAACL HLT 2018: 16th Annual Conference of the North American Chapter of the Association for Computational Linguistics: Human Language Technologies, pp. 238–251 (2018)
21. Chen, T.T., Lee, M.R.: Research paper recommender systems on big scholarly data. In: PKAW, pp. 251–260 (2018)
22. Yuan, W., et al.: Attention-based context-aware sequential recommendation model. Inf. Sci. **510**, 122–134 (2020)
23. Scarselli, F., Gori, M., Tsoi, A.C., Hagenbuchner, M., et al.: The graph neural network model. IEEE Trans. Neural Netw. **20**(1), 61–80 (2009)
24. McCallum, A.K., Nigam, K., Rennie, J., Seymore, K.: Automating the construction of internet portals with machine learning. Inf. Retrieval **3**(2), 127–163 (2000)
25. Yan, A., et al.: CosRec: 2D convolutional neural networks for sequential recommendation. In: Proceedings of the 28th ACM International Conference on Information and Knowledge Management (2019)
26. Li, Z., Ding, X., Liu, T.: Constructing narrative event evolutionary graph for script event prediction (2018)
27. Xu, C., et al.: Recurrent convolutional neural network for sequential recommendation. The World Wide Web Conference (2019)
28. Velickovic, P., Cucurull, G., Casanova, A., Romero, A., Lio, P., Bengio, Y.: Graph attention networks. In: International Conference on Learning Representations (2017)
29. Ahmadian, S., Joorabloo, N., Jalili, M., Meghdadi, M., Afsharchi, M., Ren, Y.: A temporal clustering approach for social recommender systems. In: International Conference on Advances in Social Networks Analysis and Mining (ASONAM), Barcelona, Spain, pp. 1139–1144 (2018)
30. Gohari, F.S., Aliee, F.S., Haghighi, H.: A dynamic local-global trust-aware recommendation approach. Electron. Commerce Res. Appl. **34**, 100838 (2019)

31. Wu, S., et al.: Graph neural networks in recommender systems: a survey. ACM Comput. Surv. (CSUR) (2020)
32. Guo, Q., et al.: A survey on knowledge graph-based recommender systems. IEEE Trans. Knowl. Data Eng. (2020)
33. Quadrana, M., Cremonesi, P., Jannach, D.: Sequence-aware recommender systems. ACM Comput. Surv. (CSUR) **51**(4), 1–36 (2018)

Electronic Voting Scheme Based on Blockchain and SM2 Cryptographic Algorithm Zero-Knowledge Proof

Zheng Lijuan[1,2(✉)], Li Dunyue[1], Zhang Rui[2], Zhao Yongbin[1], Feng Rouxin[1], and Chen Ziyang[1]

[1] School of Information Science and Technology,
Shijiazhuang Tiedao University, Shijiazhuang 050043, China
zhenglijuan@stdu.edu.cn

[2] State Key Laboratory of Information Security, Institute of Information Engineering,
Chinese Academy of Sciences, Beijing 100093, China

Abstract. Voting is an important basis for making decisions in social life. With the development of society, the efficiency of counting has been improved and the error rate of manual counting has been reduced by using electronic voting technology. However, the problems, such as voter information leakage, ballot reuse, and the authenticity of tallied results still exist. To solve these problems, a blockchain-based electronic voting scheme and a zero-knowledge proof protocol based on the SM2 cryptographic algorithm is proposed in this paper. Before voting, the zero-knowledge proof protocol is used to verify the voting qualification of the voter without disclosing the voter's identity. In the voting stage, a blind signature algorithm based on SM2 is used to verify the validity of the ballot and protect the privacy of the ballot information. In the counting process, the PBFT algorithm is used to ensure that the counting nodes count votes normally and produce accurate and credible counting results. Security analysis and performance analysis show that the proposed scheme meets the security requirements of the electronic voting protocol and has stronger security, privacy, and efficiency than the existing schemes.

Keywords: Blockchain · Electronic voting · Zero knowledge proof · Blind signature · SM2

1 Introduction

Voting is an important basis for making decisions in social life. The traditional voting method is time-consuming and labor-intensive [1], and cannot guarantee the fairness of voting results. Electronic voting technology was first proposed by David Chaum in 1981 [2, 3]. Compared with the traditional paper voting method, it reduces the cost of voting and the voting process is more convenient. However, the current electronic voting system is generally highly centralized and vulnerable to hackers. Secondly, voters who vote through electronic devices will be recorded with some sensitive information, and there is a risk of information leakage. In addition, the results of the voting are completely controlled by the center. There is a problem that the voting results are tampered with.

Secure electronic voting technology needs to ensure the interests of voters and the impartiality of voting results at the same time [4–6]. To this end, in 1999, Fujioka, Okamoto and Ohta [7] proposed the first protocol for large-scale voting scenarios, using blind signature and bit commitment technology to encrypt vote information before sending it to the voting management agency, effectively protecting voter privacy and ensuring the fairness of voting. However, the credibility of the voting agency cannot be guaranteed. Kiayias and Yung [8] first proposed a self-counting voting protocol for voting in board-scale scenarios; Hao et al. [9]improved it by turning the vote counting process into a publicly verifiable process, allowing any voter or third-party observers to perform the counting process after ballots are cast, reducing reliance on voting agencies. However, in this scheme, the fairness of the vote cannot be guaranteed. In 2006, Zhong Hong et al. designed a "k-out-of-m" multi-candidate voting scheme based on secure multi-party computing and no third-party trusted institutions [10], which ensures the security, confidentiality, fairness, and efficiency of ballots. In 2012, Sun Peiyong et al. [11], based on this document [10], used random numbers to blindly process votes to ensure the confidentiality of vote information but still could not ensure that the results of vote counting were completely credible. Liu Gao et al. [12] proposed an electronic voting scheme based on the discrete logarithm difficulty problem in 2015, which ensures the authenticity of the vote counting process and the result of the vote counting is verifiable.

Although the above scheme guarantees the complete confidentiality of the votes and the authenticity of the vote counting, once the central node is maliciously attacked, the personal information of the voters will be leaked, which will affect the results of the votes, and the results of the votes will be tampered with. With the development of blockchain technology, many researchers have combined their research with blockchain to propose new electronic voting schemes. Zhao et al. [13] proposed a Bitcoin-based electronic voting scheme in 2015. Protect voters' personal information. A penalty mechanism is introduced, and nodes that violate the protocol need to pay a certain amount of compensation. In 2016, Lee et al. [14] proposed a blockchain-based electronic voting scheme to ensure the validity of voting through the participation of trusted third parties. Cruz and Kaji [15] proposed an electronic voting protocol based on the Bitcoin protocol and blind signatures. In the proposed system, voters need to handle an additional key, the private key of the Bitcoin address used to vote. The results are only credible if all entities participating in the voting are honest.

The above schemes require the participation of a trusted third party, and the trusted third party must be completely honest. If a third party colludes with voting participants to attack, it will affect the fairness of voting. Since the voting process is not completely anonymous, even if the voter does not use completely real identity information, some real information can still be guessed through chaining attacks [16, 17]. McCorry [18] and others proposed an electronic voting scheme based on Ethereum in 2017. The function of self-counting is realized through smart contracts, and a trusted third-party counting agency is not required. Enhanced privacy protection for voters. Reference [19] proposed an electronic voting scheme based on consortium chain, which is suitable for anonymous voting by a small group of a specific range. The blind signature algorithm is adopted, and smart contracts are used to replace traditional third-party institutions, which ensures the anonymity of voting. Reference [20] adopts Elgamal strong blind signature, which reduces the correlation between voter information and signature, improves the anonymity of votes, and protects the personal information of voters and candidates. Reference [21] proposes a blockchain electronic voting scheme based on one-time ring signature, which solves the problems of voter anonymity, repeated voting, and public verification. Reference [22] proposes a new blind signature algorithm based on the national commercial cryptographic algorithm SM2, which realizes strong blindness, and can effectively resist the adaptive selection of messages under the random oracle model. Existential forgery attack. Reference [23] proposes an electronic voting protocol based on Ethereum, which adopts the distributed ElGamal encryption system and zero-knowledge proof. Through two rounds of zero-knowledge proofs, it ensures the protection of voter privacy, verification of identity and legitimacy of votes.

The research of the above scheme rely on smart contracts to complete the process of self-counting. However, due to the possible existence of dishonest nodes, the final result of voting cannot be guaranteed to be reliable.Based on the above problems, this paper will propose a new blockchain-based electronic voting scheme. The main research work is as follows: (1) Combining the SM2 cryptographic algorithm elliptic curve algorithm with the non-interactive zero-knowledge proof protocol. Through this zero-knowledge proof protocol before voting, the voter's voting eligibility is verified without revealing the voter's identity, and the voter's identity information is protected. (2) Based on the blind signature algorithm of the SM2, the voter's vote is signed in the voting stage. Only the signed vote can be recorded in the result as a valid vote in the vote counting stage, and each vote can only be signed. Once, the ballot is guaranteed not to be used again. Due to the blind signature mechanism, the management subsystem in the scheme, as the signer, cannot know the ballot information, which ensures that the ballot information will not be leaked. (3) Use the PBFT algorithm as a consensus protocol between blockchain nodes. In the vote counting stage, even if there are dishonest nodes, as long as there are enough honest nodes working normally, the vote counting process and results can still be guaranteed to be true and reliable, get rid of the dependence on the voting center, and prevent the voting organization from Absolute control of statistical results.

2 Electronic Voting Scheme Based on Blockchain and Zero-Knowledge Proof of SM2

2.1 Solution Model

In this scheme, a new blockchain-based electronic voting scheme is proposed. Adopt the alliance chain to realize the electronic voting scheme, and introduce zero-knowledge proof, blind signature and PBFT algorithm to meet the requirements of electronic voting security. This scheme includes the following subjects: administrators, voters, registration subsystems, management subsystems and consensus nodes. The scheme model is shown in Fig. 1.

Administrators are responsible for creating polling events and setting up polling-related information. The administrator does not participate in the voting, and is only responsible for publishing the relevant content of the voting. The administrators are jointly selected by voters before each poll begins.

Voters participate in the voting within the specified time, or cast their ballots, or choose to abstain. Voters will be verified for eligibility to vote before voting begins.

Registration subsystem: After the administrator has set the relevant information for voting, the voter completes the registration in the registration subsystem, and after the registration is completed, a certificate is sent to the voter, indicating that he or she is eligible to vote.

Management subsystem: Before the voting session, the management subsystem verifies the identity of the voter. After the verification is completed, the voter's ballot is blindly signed to make it a valid ballot.

Consensus node: After the voting session ends, collect the votes of all voters, verify the validity of all votes, count the information of the votes, and publish them on the blockchain after reaching a consensus.

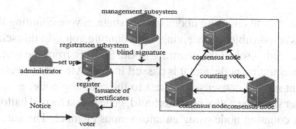

Fig. 1. Blockchain-based electronic voting scheme model

2.2 Solution Process

The scheme process is divided into five stages: initialization stage, registration stage, prevoting stage, voting stage and vote counting stage, as shown in Fig. 2. The participants of this voting scheme mainly include N eligible voters $(C_1, C_2, C_3, \ldots, C_n)$, for multiple candidates$(v_1, v_2, v_3, \ldots, v_n)$to conduct multi-election and multi-form voting.

(1) Initialization: The voting initiator and the voters negotiate a manager. The manager uploads the relevant information of the candidates, and generates the hash identification for the legitimate voters. Set the candidate list $\{\{v_i | v_i \in N\}$, the legal voter list $List_{vote}$, the registration end time $T_{registerF}$, the voting start time T_{voteB}, the voting end time T_{votrF}, and the elliptic curve parameters used for setting $\{F_q, E(F_q), G, q, SM3\}$. The manager runs the blockchain platform, deploys smart contracts, and informs voters that the initialization phase has been completed.

(2) Registration stage:voters generate random numbers x_i, $x_i \subset Z_n^*$, calculate public key $y_i = x_i G$; public public key, calculate $c = hash(G_x, y_{ix})$, $r = x_i - x_i c$,Send r to the registration subsystem; the registration subsystem verifies whether $P*c + G*r = P$ holds, and uses $\{r, y_i, y_{ix}\}$ as the proof information. The registration subsystem generates the management subsystem key (k, Y), and sends k to the management

subsystem through a secure channel. It is assumed that the secure channel can protect the confidentiality and integrity of information.

(3) Pre-voting stage:The voter selects the candidate $v_i \in \{v_1, \ldots v_n\}$, $1 \le i \le n$, executes the BlindM algorithm to generate the blind message m_i', and sends it to the management subsystem together with the proof information. The management subsystem receives the blinded message and verifies the proof information, if the proof information is valid. Verify that the information is correct. If it is the first time to sign, sign it, execute the BlindS algorithm to get s_i', and send it to the voter. Otherwise, the visa will be refused.

(4) Voting stage: the voter receives the blindly signed ballot s_i', and executes the UnblindM algorithm to obtain the official ballot m_i. Voters send official ballots to counting nodes.

(5) Voting counting stage: electing a counting node, which collects official votes, verifies the validity of the votes, counts the votes, and after reaching a consensus, publishes the counting results and stores the results on the blockchain.

1) Election of vote counting node: In this stage, a vote counting node is elected, which is responsible for receiving and counting votes. In this scheme, a random token is used to select the counting node. Starting from the first node $Node_1$, it acts as a counting node, and it is passed in turn. After the selection is complete, the client sends a consensus request to the counting node;

2) The voter signs the ballot m_i in his hand, generates a formal ballot, and transmits it to the counting node using an anonymous channel. The vote counting node uses the public key Y to perform the BlindVer algorithm to verify the signature and count votes if true;

3) Pre-preparation stage: The vote counting node acts as the master node to send the results of counting votes to other nodes, indicating that the consensus is about to start. Other nodes accept the message after receiving the message;

4) Preparation stage: After receiving the message, the non-voting node sends the vote result and the hash value calculated by itself to other nodes. Since multiple nodes are executing the process, the node will receive the message sent by other nodes.The current node needs to confirm whether the hash value and voting results of these messages are consistent with the current voting node. Within a certain period of time, if more than 2f of other nodes' messages are acknowledged, the phase is complete. The voting node sends the hash of the voting result as a commit message;

5) Confirmation phase: Receive commit messages from more than 2f other nodes within a certain period of time, and verify whether the commit messages sent by these nodes are consistent with this node. After the verification is successful, at least f + 1 nodes in the entire system have reached a consensus on the message m. The vote counting node returns f + 1 messages to the client, the consensus is completed, and the voting result is released.

Within the specified time, if the counting node does not send a pre-prepare message, or does not send a commit message, or does not return a message to the client after receiving the request from the client, it will re-elect a new counting node. 3) Start over.

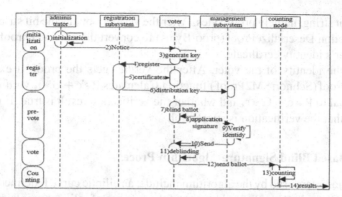

Fig. 2. Flow chart of electronic voting scheme based on blockchain

2.3 SM2-Based Zero-Knowledge Proof Protocol

This scheme introduces the SM2 algorithm into the discrete logarithmic proof protocol to ensure that voters prove to the system that they hold valid private information without revealing this private information. The process is shown in Fig. 3, and the detailed steps are as follows:

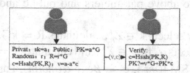

Fig. 3. Zero-knowledge proof process based on SM2 Cryptographic Algorithm

(1) Initialization: Execute the GenerateKey() function, use the random number generator to generate an integer $d \in [1, n - 2]$, G is the base point, the calculation point $P = (XP, YP) = [d]G$, the key pair is (d, P), where d is the private key, P is the public key, and the key is distributed to voters.

(2) Build challenges. Before voting, voters execute createChallenge (PublicKey,PrivateKey)$\rightarrow$ (c,a,n) input parameters (PublicKey, PrivateKey), and get parameters c, a, n, then PublicKey = {P, Curve}, PrivateKey = {PublicKey, d, Curve}. Curve is a collection of elliptic curve related parameter information used. $c = H(Gx, Px)$, $a = Px$, n is one of the elliptic curve parameters.

(3) Construct the zero-knowledge identity proof of the voter. The voter executes CreateProof() $\rightarrow$ SchnorrSM2Proof, SchnorrSM2Proof is a set containing the zero-knowledge identity proof of the voter, SchnorrSM2Proof = {r, P, PA}. Where $r = d - dc$.

(4) Serialization and deserialization of voter's identity certificate. During the transmission of the identity certificate, it needs to be transmitted in the form of a bit string, execute the SerializeProof(SchnorrSM2Proof) function, and convert the certificate

into a bit string, namely proofBytes. After the verifier obtains the bit string, execute the function DeserializeProof(proofBytes) to convert the obtained proofBytes into the voter's identity certificate.

(5) Verify the identity of the voter. After the verifier gets the proof, it executes the VerifyProof(SchnorrSM2Proof) function.Calculates $P*c+G*r$, verifies whether P is equal to $P*c+G*r$, and whether the verification result is true. If it is true, it means that the verification is successful.

2.4 SM2-Based Blind Signature Algorithm Process

The main parameters used by the algorithm include: an elliptic curve E defined on a finite field GF(q), GF(q) is characterized by p, and the number of rational points of GF(q) on E is divisible by a large prime number n. A base point $G \in ((GF(q)))$ can be written as: D = (q, FR, a, b, G, n, h), (d, Q), SM3

Where q is the number of elements in the finite field; FR is the representation method of the elements in the finite field; a, b $\in$ GF(q), , the curve on GF(q) is defined as: $y = x^3 + ax + b, p > 3 y^2 + xy = x^3 + ax^2 + b, p = 2$

n is a prime number, $n > 2^{160}$ and $n > 4\sqrt{q}$, n is the order of G, h is called the cofactor.Hash function SM3 : $\{0, 1\}^* \rightarrow \{0, 1\}^{256}$ is a cryptographic hash function standard adopted in my country. Make D = (q, FR, a, b, G, n, h), Q, SM3 public and d secret. Signer S uses the above parameters and public and private keys to sign the following message m:

The signer S randomly selects $k \in Z_n^*$, calculates R = kG, and then passes R to the user.The user randomly selects $\alpha, \beta, \gamma \in Z_n^*$, and calculates $F = \beta^{-1}Q + \alpha\beta^{-1}R + \gamma G = (x, y)$, $f = x(mod n)$, $c = SM3(mf)$, $c' = \beta c + \alpha(mod n)$. Pass c' to signer S.

Signer S computes $s' = dc' + k(mod n)$ and passes s' to user U.User U calculates $s = \beta^{-1}s' + \gamma(mod n)$ to generate a signature (c, s) for message m.

Signature verification: just verify $sQ - cG = \beta^{-1}Q + \alpha\beta^{-1}R + \gamma G$

$$sG - cQ = (s - cd)G = \left(\left(\beta^{-1}s' + \gamma\right) - cd\right)G$$

$$= \left(\left(\beta^{-1}(d(\beta c + \alpha) + k) + \gamma\right) - cd\right)G = \left(dc + \beta^{-1}d\alpha + \beta^{-1}k + \gamma\right)G - cQ$$

$$= \beta^{-1}Q + \alpha\beta^{-1}R + \gamma G$$

It can be verified that s is a blind signature for message m.

3 Safety Analysis

3.1 Security Analysis of Blind Signature Algorithm Based on SM2

Proof of unforgeability: This scheme makes security proofs from its unforgeability. By definition, the unforgeability of a scheme can be described as a game in which an adversary (hereinafter referred to as A) plays a game with a challenger [24–26]. After the adversary and the challenger get fixed key parameters, the adversary needs to generate a valid signature for the message m^* selected by the challenger [27, 28]. The whole scheme consists of six parts: parameter generation (Setup), key generation (GetKey), blind conversion message (BlindM), signature (BlindS), blind elimination (UnblindM) and signature verification (BlindVer). Unforgeable games are defined as follows:

(1) Initialization: The challenger executes the Setup function to generate system parameters: $(F_q, E(F_q), G, n, q, H)$ Then the challenger runs the key generation algorithm GetKey to get the key pair $(k,R),(d,Q)$,then the challenger chooses a message m^*.

(2) BlindM query: A adaptively requests q_b messages $\{m_1, \ldots\ldots m_{q_b}\}$, the challenger returns the BlindM blind message pair (c_i, c_i'), $i \in \{1, \ldots\ldots q_b\}$.

(3) BlindS query: A requests q_s blinded messages $\{c_1', \ldots\ldots c_{1q_s}'\}$ to the challenger, and the challenger returns the BlindS blinded signature s_i', $i \in \{1, \ldots\ldots q_s\}$.

(4) UnblindM query: A requests q_r blinded signatures $\{s_1', \ldots\ldots s_{1q_r}'\}$ from the challenger, and the challenger returns the UnblindM unblinded signature s_i, $i \in \{1, \ldots\ldots q_r\}$.

(5) Output: A outputs a signature pair (c^*, s^*), if the message signature (m^*, c^*, s^*) can be verified by the BlindVer algorithm, then A wins.

Theorem 1: Under the random oracle model, if there is an adversary A that can successfully destroy the unforgeability of the ECDSA (Elliptic Curve Digital Signature Algorithm) [29, 30] scheme with a non-negligible probability ε in polynomial time, then there is a challenger who can also use the unforgeable The ignored probability solves the ECDLP (Elliptic Curve Discrete Logarithm Problem) [31] problem in polynomial time in $\varepsilon \bullet (1 - 1/n)^{q_b + q_s}$. The probability ε of the adversary winning is defined as the adversary's advantage. If the adversary's advantage is negligible in this scheme, then the scheme is unforgeable.

Proof: In polynomial time, assuming that A can perform at most q_b BlindM queries, the challenger randomly selects the challenge target m^*, $m^* \in [0, n - 1]$. If A can win the unforgeability game, then the challenger can solve the ECDLP problem by giving A as a subroutine[32].

The following is the interaction process between A and the challenger:

(1) The challenger performs the initialization step and generates the challenge message m^*. Then execute the BlindM algorithm to generate the blinded message m_*', and then send the challenge target message m^* to A.

(2) Inquiry stage: BlindM inquiry phase: The challenger maintains a list $List_b$ with empty values and fields $\{m_i, \alpha_i, \beta_i, \gamma_i, c_i, c_i'\}$. When A submits a BlindM query request about m_i, if $m_i = m^*$, the challenger returns $\perp$ and terminates the query process; otherwise, the challenger queries the $List_b$ list.If there is a corresponding record in the $List_b$ list $\{m_i, \alpha_i, \beta_i, \gamma_i, c_i, c_i'\}$, then return $\{m_i, c_i, c_i'\}$ to A; if there is no corresponding item, the challenger will execute BlindM query, update $List_b$, and set $\{m_i, c_i, c_i'\}$ returns to A.

2) BlindS inquiry phase: The challenger maintains a list $List_s$ whose initial value is empty and the field is $\left\{m_i, c_i', s_i'\right\}$. When A submits a BlindS query about $\left\{m_i, c_i'\right\}$, if $m_i = m^*$ or $c_i' = c'^*$, the challenger returns $\perp$ and terminates the query process. Otherwise, the challenger queries the list $List_s$, if it matches the corresponding $\left\{m_i, c_i', s_i'\right\}$, send s_i' to A. If the corresponding record cannot be found, the challenger executes BlindS query and sends s_i' Give A, and update the list $List_s$.

3) UnblindM inquiry stage: The challenger maintains a list $List_r$ whose initial value is empty and whose fields are $\left\{m_i, s_i', s_i\right\}$. When A submits an UnblindM query about $\left\{m_i, s_i'\right\}$. If $m_i = m^*$, the challenger returns $\perp$. If $m_i \neq m^*$, the challenger queries $List_r$. If there is a corresponding record, then Return s_i to A; otherwise, the challenger executes the UnblindM query. Generates s_i and returns it to A and updates the list $List_r$.

(3) Output stage: A terminates the query and outputs the message signature pair (m^*, c^*, s^*), if $m^* \notin \left\{m_1, \ldots \ldots m_{q_b}\right\}$, and it can pass the BlindVer algorithm, then this game A wins.

At this time, the challenger can use the bifurcation lemma[33], select different random numbers α_i, β_i, γ_i, and then simulate with A to generate a valid signature pair $\left(c_2^*, s_2^*\right)$. According to $sQ - cG = \beta^{-1}Q + \alpha\beta^{-1}R + \gamma G$ and $R = kG$, $Q = dG$, there is the following formula:

$$r^*Q - c^*G = \beta_1^{-1}Q + \alpha_1\beta_1^{-1}R + \gamma_1 G; \quad s_2^*Q - c_2^*G = \beta_2^{-1}Q + \alpha_2\beta_2^{-1}R + \gamma_2 G$$

There are only two unknown variables k and d in the equation. The simultaneous equations can obtain the values of k and d, and the challenger can solve the ECDLP problem.

Since A performs at most q_b BlindM queries and q_s BlindS queries, and $m^* \in [1, q_b]$, the probability that A does not use m^* to perform BlindM queries is $((1 - 1/n)^{q_b}$, The probability that A does not use c'^* for BlindM query is $(1 - 1/n)^{q_s}$. If A destroys the unforgeability of ECBDSA with non-negligible probability ε in polynomial time, then challenger C succeeds with probability $\varepsilon' = \varepsilon \bullet (1 - 1/n)^{q_b+q_s}$. Therefore, if the probability of A successfully forging the signature pair (c^*, s^*) is non-negligible, the challenger is able to solve the ECDLP puzzle with a non-negligible advantage ε'. To sum up, the elliptic curve blind signature scheme is unforgeable.

Strong blinding analysis: In this scheme, the signer performs blind transformation on the message that needs to be signed, so it can be determined that the plaintext message m is invisible to the signer, so the scheme satisfies weak blindness. The signature information stored by the signer is (k, d, Q, f, c', s'). When the user discloses the message signature pair (m, (c, s)), the signer also obtains the signature information. If the signer wants to associate any message signature pair (m, (c, s)) with the saved blind transform message signature pair, he needs to solve the system of equations:

$$c' = \beta^{-1}f^{-1}(c - \alpha),\ s' = \beta(s - \gamma),\ sQ - cG = \beta^{-1}Q + \alpha\beta^{-1}R + \gamma G$$

The signer will be faced with solving the elliptic curve discrete logarithm problem over a finite field. To sum up, the strong blindness of this scheme can be reduced to the ECDLP problem on finite fields, so this scheme has strong blindness.

Analysis of effectiveness: Theorem 2: (c, s) is a valid signature for message m, and can be obtained from Strong blinding analysis, this scheme has strong blindness. According to the signature steps:

$$sG - cQ = (s - cd)G = \left(\left(\beta^{-1}\left(dc' + k\right) + \gamma\right) - cd\right)G$$

$$= cQ + \beta^{-1}Q + \alpha\beta^{-1}R + \gamma G - cQ = \beta^{-1}Q + \alpha\beta^{-1}R + \gamma G$$

So (c, s) in this scheme is a valid signature of message m.

Analysis of non-repudiation: It can be seen from Theorem 1 that, except for the signer, any polynomial-time adversary cannot forge the blind signature of the signer, trying to obtain the private key information k, d by solving $s' = dc' + k(mod n)$, must face the difficult problem of solving ECDLP. So if a pair of signatures $(m'', (c'', s''))$ passes the verification algorithm, the signer cannot deny that the private key k and d are used to sign the message m'''. It can be seen that the scheme is non-repudiation.

3.2 Scheme Security Analysis

This paper proposes a blockchain electronic voting scheme based on SM2. The voting process can be publicly verifiable and data tamper-proof. The following is a security analysis of the voting system in the following aspects:

(1) Complete confidentiality of votes: This scheme uses a zero-knowledge proof protocol based on SM2 Cryptographic Algorithm to verify the identity of voters. The validator cannot obtain the relevant private information of the voter. By blindly signing the ballot, the signer cannot know the content of the signature, and cannot distinguish the signatures for different ballots, which ensures the complete confidentiality of the ballot information. Collecting, validating and counting votes are all performed by smart contracts. The running results of smart contracts will be written into the ledger and made public. The identity and voting information of the voter cannot be determined even if the attacker obtains the data of the voter.

(2) Fairness: After all voters have sent their voting results within the specified voting time, the system's smart contract can verify and count votes. Therefore, as long as there are voters who did not send their ballots in the correct time, the voting results cannot be known in advance. Therefore, the scheme is fair.

(3) Non-controversial: The scheme needs to verify the voting eligibility of voters before voting. Each ballot has the attribute of the number of signatures, which limits the number of times the ballot can be used. One person can only cast one vote, and one vote can only select one candidate. This ensures the accuracy of the voting results, and the voting scheme is non-controversial.

(4) Verifiability: After the voter submits the ballot, he can check the relevant information of the confirmed ballot in his registered account before the system counts the voting results. After the statistical results come out, every voter can check the information of the ballots and calculate whether the results of the counting are consistent with the published results.

(5) Eligibility: In this scheme, all voters are given identification information after registration is completed. Before voting, it is necessary to authenticate the identity information of the voter to ensure that the voters participating in the vote are legitimate. The ballot needs to be blindly signed by the management subsystem to generate the official ballot, and all the ballots participating in the final vote count are also legal.

(6) Robustness: During the voting process of the scheme, you can choose to abstain from voting. Those who still do not cast a vote after the specified time will be regarded as abstaining and enter the voting process. Even if there are uncooperative voters, it will not affect the normal conduct of voting. The vote counting process reaches a consensus through PBFT, so even if there is a faulty node, it will not affect the normal operation of the vote counting process.

(7) Self-counting: In the process of counting votes, the scheme uses a smart contract program to replace the role of a third-party counting agency, and does not require the participation of a third-party counting agency. Using zero-knowledge proof and blind signature cryptography technology, the legitimacy of the voter and the legitimacy of the vote are verified to ensure that the voting scheme proposed in this paper is carried out in accordance with the characteristics of self-counting.

To sum up, the electronic voting scheme designed in this paper meets the security requirements, protects the private information of voters to the greatest extent, and ensures the fairness and verifiability of the voting results.

4 Scheme Analysis

4.1 Performance Analysis

In order to verify the correctness and effectiveness of this scheme, the overall time-consuming of the scheme is calculated by changing the number of voters and candidates, as shown in the left of Fig. 4. In the case of a large increase in voters, as shown on the right in Fig. 4. The test environment is: ubuntu18.04, 4GB memory. In order to simulate a real voting scenario, an odd number of voters were chosen. The overall time-consuming of the scheme is basically linearly related to the number of people participating in the vote. Changing the number of candidates has little effect on the overall time-consuming of the scheme, so the scheme in this paper can meet the requirements of basic voting scenarios.

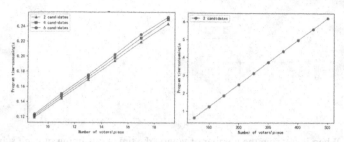

Fig. 4. Overall time spent with different voter numbers.

4.2 Performance Comparison

The proposed scheme is compared with reference [20], reference [21], reference [22] and reference [23] under the condition that the fixed number of candidates is 6. As shown in Fig. 5. The fixed number of candidates is 20, and the number of voting participants is increased, as shown in Fig. 6. When the fixed number of voting participants is 100, changing the number of candidates will take time to calculate the scheme. As shown in Fig. 7.

Reference [20] adopts the Elgamal blind signature algorithm, which is higher than the SM2 blind signature algorithm used in reference [22] in terms of algorithm efficiency. This is because the SM2 blind signature algorithm proposed by the literature [22] uses three random blind factors, which increases the overall time consumption, but improves the security. In [21], with the increase of the number of voters, the time-consuming increases rapidly. This is because as the number of voters increases, it becomes more difficult for the ring signature algorithm to generate rings. Reference [23] adopts two rounds of zero-knowledge proof protocol, and the time consumption is basically the same as this scheme. This scheme uses a round of zero-knowledge proof protocol to verify the identity of the voter and a new SM2 blind signature algorithm to ensure the privacy of votes. Compared with the reference [22], it reduces the number of public and private keys generated, thereby reducing the overall time-consuming of the scheme. It is more secure than reference [20] and reference [22]. To sum up, while ensuring security, this scheme reduces the overall time-consuming of the scheme and improves the efficiency of the electronic voting scheme.

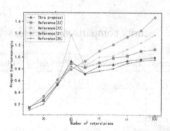

Fig. 5. Overall time-consuming comparison of five schemes.

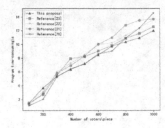

Fig. 6. When increasing the number of voters, the time-consuming of each schemes.

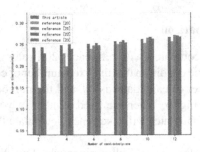

Fig. 7. When the number of candidates is different, the time-consuming of each schemes.

4.3 Security Comparison

This scheme is compared with reference [20], reference [21], reference [22] and reference [23] in terms of system security. As shown in Table 1.

Reference [20] uses a strong blind signature algorithm based on Elgamal, which reduces the correlation between the voter's identity and the signature, and protects the privacy of voters and candidates.It realizes automatic counting of votes.. The introduction of unlinkable payment technology makes the public key of the transaction recipient irreversible. Reference [21] proposes a one-time ring signature-based blockchain electronic voting scheme. By introducing a one-time ring signature, the problems of voter anonymity, repeated voting, and public verification are solved. The openness and transparency of the voting process is solved through blockchain technology. Use anonymous address technology to ensure that the voting results are not controversial.

Table 1. Security comparison of voting schemes.

Scheme	Confidentiality	Fairness	Uncontroversial	Verifiability	Eligibility	Robustness	Self-counting
This article	✓	✓	✓	✓	✓	✓	✓
Reference [20]	✓	✓	✓	×	×	×	✓
Reference [21]	✓	✓	✓	×	×	✓	–
Reference [22]	✓	✓	✓	✓	✓	×	✓
Reference [23]	✓	✓	✓	✓	×	×	✓

Reference [22] proposed a new blind signature algorithm based on the SM2, which achieved strong blindness and ensured that the signed information would not be leaked. It meets the security requirements of the blind signature algorithm, and can effectively resist the existence forgery attack under the adaptive selection message under the random oracle model. By way of self-counting. Reference [23] proposes an electronic voting protocol based on Ethereum, which adopts the distributed ElGamal encryption system and zero-knowledge proof. The first round of zero-knowledge proof protocol is a discrete logarithmic knowledge proof protocol, which is used to verify the identity information of voters. The second round of the zero-knowledge proof protocol is the legitimacy knowledge proof protocol, which verifies that the voter has indeed cast a vote. The self-counting method is adopted to avoid the situation that the counting agency controls the voting results.

Reference [20] and [21] before the statistics of the system voting results are completed, the voters who have voted cannot view their personal voting information on the voting platform, which does not satisfy the verifiability. Eligibility. Reference [20] does not design voting time and abstention options. If there are uncooperative voters, it will affect the normal voting, which is not robust. In the vote counting process of reference [22] and reference [23], if there are malicious nodes and faulty nodes, it will have an impact on the consensus process, resulting in lower efficiency. Too many numbers will even affect the vote counting results, and the robustness is relatively high. Difference. Reference [23] does not design the verification link of ballots, and there is a situation of reuse of ballots, which is not qualified.

The blockchain-based electronic voting scheme proposed in this paper adopts a SM2-based zero-knowledge proof protocol and a blind signature algorithm. Before the voting stage to ensure that the voter's private information is not leaked. In the voting session, a new SM2 blind signature algorithm is used to blindly sign the ballots, and generate valid ballots while protecting the ballot information from being leaked. The self-counting method is adopted, and PBFT is used as the consensus algorithm, and only one third of the summary points are needed to reach a consensus to release the voting result. This scheme satisfies the security requirements of an electronic voting scheme and has practical significance.

5 Conclusion

The application of electronic voting technology is beneficial to reduce the cost of voting, facilitate the voting method, and obtain more accurate and true voting results. But with the continuous development of information technology. Electronic voting technology faces the problems of leakage of voter information, tampering of ballot information, secondary reuse of ballots, and untrue voting results. It seriously affects the principles of fairness, openness and impartiality in voting. This paper combines blockchain technology, zero-knowledge proof protocol and elliptic curve blind signature technology with electronic voting, and proposes a blockchain-based electronic voting scheme. Through the security proof, security analysis, experimental comparison and scheme comparison, it is shown that this scheme can ensure that the voter's identity can be verified before the voting stage while protecting the voter's private information, the vote information is protected in the voting stage, and the vote counting result can be ensured in the vote counting process. of authenticity. This solution can be implemented more safely and reliably.

Acknowledgement. This research was partially supported by the State Key Laboratory of Information Security Open Project (No. 2021-MS-09); Provincial Postgraduate Demonstration Course (No. KCJSX2021055); Science and Technology Project of Colleges and Universities of Hebei Province(NO. ZD2020174); Shijiazhuang Tiedao University Postgraduate Innovation Funding Project (NO. YC2022054, NO. YC2022070).

References

1. Chaum, D.: Untraceable electronic mail, return address, and digital pseudonyms. Commun. ACM. **28**(2), 84–88 (1981)
2. Nakamoto, S.: Bitcoin: a peer-to-peer electronic cash system. www.bitcoin.org (2008)
3. Goldwasser, S., Micali, S., Rackoff, C.: The knowledge complexity of interactive proof systems. SIAM J. Comput. **18**, 186–208 (1989)
4. Bunz, B., et al.: Bulletproofs: Short Proofs for Confidential Transactions and More. IEEE Symposium on Security and Privacy, pp. 315–334 (2018)
5. Uzma, J., Ab, A.M.J., Zarina, S.: Blockchain for electronic voting system—review and open research challenges. Sensors **21**(17), 5874 (2021)
6. JaeGeun, S., SungJun, M., JuWook, J.: A scalable implementation of anonymous voting over ethereum blockchain. Sensors **21**(12), 3958 (2021)
7. Fujioka, A., Okamoto, T., Ohta, K.: A practical secret voting scheme for large scale elections. In: ProcAuscrypt92 Gold Coast Queensland Australia, vol. 718, pp. 244–251 (December 1992)
8. Kiayias, A., Yung, M.: Self-tallying elections and perfect ballot secrecy. In: International Workshop on Public Key Cryptography, pp. 141–158. Springer (2002). https://doi.org/10.1007/3-540-45664-3_10
9. Hao, F., Ryan, P.Y.A., Zielinski, P.: Anonymous voting by two-round public discussion. IET Inf. Secur. **4**(2), 62–67 (2010)
10. Zhong, H., Huang, L., Luo, Y.: A multi-candidate electronic voting scheme based on secure sum protocol. J. Comput. Res. Dev. **43**(8), 1405–1410 (2006)
11. Sun, P., Liu, Y., Yan, J.: Secure E-voting scheme with multi-candidates. Comput. Eng. Appl. **48**(25), 217–219 (2012)
12. Liu, G., Liu, Y.N., Wang, D.: A verifiable e-voting scheme with multi-candidates. Comput. Eng. Sci. **37**(9), 1667–1670 (2015)
13. Zhao, Z., Chan, T.: How to vote privately using bitcoin. In: International Conference on Information & Communications Security. Springer International Publishing, Cham (2015)
14. Ma, S., Deng, Y., He, D., Zhang, J., Xie, X.: An efficient NIZK scheme for privacy-preserving transactions over account-model blockchain. IEEE Trans. Dependable Secure Comput. **18**(2), 641–651 (2021)
15. Jason, P.C., Yuichi, K.: E-voting system based on the bitcoin protocol and blind signatures. Trans. Math. Model. Appl. **10**(1), 14–22 (2017)
16. Yu, T., Cao, C., Wang, L., Xu, L.: Anonymous electronic voting scheme based on alliance chain. Cyberspace Secur. **10**(12), 22–29 (2019)
17. Hongquan, P., Zhe, C., Ting, L., Jintao, R.: Research review of secure electronic voting scheme. Comput. Sci. **47**(09), 275–282 (2020)

18. Mccorry, P., Shahandashti, S.F., Hao, F.: A Smart Contract for Boardroom Voting with Maximum Voter Privacy. Springer, Cham (2017)
19. Youkang, D., Dawei, Z., Zhen, H., Liang, C.: Electronic voting system for board of directors based on alliance blockchain. J. Net. Inform. Secur. 3(12), 17–23 (2017)
20. Shao, Q., Hong, H., Li, B.: Research on blockchain electronic voting scheme based on Elgamal strong blind signature. In: Small Microcomputer System, pp. 1–8. http://kns.cnki.net/kcms/detail/21.1106.TP.20201231.1350.008.html (3 November 2021)
21. Lai, H.: Research and Design of Anonymous Electronic Voting Scheme Based on Blockchain. Jiangxi University of Science and Technology (2020)
22. Dong, Y.: Design and Implementation of a Secure Electronic Voting System Based on Blockchain. Beijing Jiaotong University (2019)
23. Yan, C.: Research and Design of Secure Voting System Based on Blockchain. Hangzhou Dianzi University (2018)
24. Weihan, L., Zongyang, Z., Zibo, Z., Yi, D.: A survey of concise non-interactive zero-knowledge proofs. J. Cryptogr. 9(03), 379–447 (2022). https://doi.org/10.13868/j.cnki.jcr.000525
25. Chao, L., Xinyi, H., Debiao, H.: Efficient range proof protocol based on SM2. J. Comput. Sci. 45(01), 148–159 (2022)
26. Ishai, Y., et al.: Zero-knowledge proofs from secure multiparty computation. SIAM J. Comput. 39(3), 1121–1152 (2009)
27. Abdolmaleki, B., Lipmaa, H., Siim, J., Zając, M.: On subversion-resistant SNARKs. J. Cryptol. 34(3), 1–42 (2021). https://doi.org/10.1007/s00145-021-09379-y
28. Yatao, Y., Yang, Z., Qilin, Z., Yingjie, M., Yuan, G.: Homomorphic weighted electronic voting system based on SEAL library. Chin. J. Comput. 43(04), 711–723 (2020)
29. Yawei, L., Weiqiong, W., Qiong, X.: Multi-candidate electronic voting scheme based on secure multi-party computing. Comput. Syst. Appl. 31(04), 386–391 (2022). https://doi.org/10.15888/j.cnki.csa.008421
30. Xuefeng, Z., Hua, P.: Research on a blind signature scheme based on SM9 algorithm. Inform. Net. Secur. 08, 61–67 (2019)
31. Tao, G., Zhitang, L., Peng Jianfen, W., Shizhong.: Blind signature and offline electronic cash protocol based on elliptic curve. J. Commun. 09, 142–146 (2003)
32. Pointcheval, D., Stern, J.: Security arguments for digital signatures and blind signatures. J. Cryptol. 13(3), 361–396 (2000)
33. Goldwasser, S., Micali, S., Rivest, R.L.: A digital signature scheme secure against adaptive chosen-message attacks. SIAM J. Comput. 17(2), 281–308 (1988)

Web 3.0: Developments and Directions of the Future Internet Architecture?

Yuchao Zhang[(✉)] , Pengmiao Li, Peizhuang Cong, Huan Zou,
Xiaotian Wang, and Xiaofeng He

Beijing University of Posts and Telecommunications, Beijing, China
yczhang@bupt.edu.cn

Abstract. As a promising emerging technology, Web3.0 has become the focus of more and more manufacturers and researchers. Web3.0 is an integration of network readability, writability, and authenticity. It is not only a new Internet architecture that integrates multiple rising technologies based on decentralization, but also an Internet infrastructure owned and trusted by each individual users. It reshapes the relationship between users and applications, by storing data on the network, rather than on specific servers owned by large service providers, which means that anyone can use this data without creating access credentials or obtaining permission from those monopolistic providers. This vision paper will first review the way the current network services work, then introduce some key technologies closely related to Web3.0, and finally point out the future research directions and potential opportunities, which are expected to give researchers a better understanding of Web3.0.

Keywords: Web3.0 · Storage · Transmission · BlockChain · CrossChain · Decentralized identity · Federated learning · Security

1 Introduction

In the past several decades, the Internet has been developing along with the development of storage, computing and transmission. Our current network built based on TCP/IP provides web services via http(s). Service or application providers usually first collect user registration information, and then store all the data (generated from users or required by users) in cloud data centers, they design data transmission algorithms to realize data synchronization across their multiple datacenters, and provide low latency services by using edge caching.

The work was supported in part by the Key Project of Beijing Natural Science Foundation under M21030, the National Natural Science Foundation of China(NSFC) under Grant 62172054, and the National Key R&D Program of China under Grant 2019YFB1802603.
P. Li, P. Cong, H. Zou, X. Wang and X. He—Authors contribute equally to this paper.

Y. Zhang and L.-J. Zhang (Eds.): ICWS 2022, LNCS 13736, pp. 104–121, 2022.
https://doi.org/10.1007/978-3-031-23579-5_8

Compared with Web1.0, where users can only passively receive information, Web2.0 service mode allows users to interact with network, but the core of it is strong centralization, including centralized identity authentication and centralized data storage. This leads to efficient network management, but also brings the following drawbacks to the current network: 1) fragile authentication: simple (or encrypted) password checking to confirm user identity and access rights, 2) un-guaranteed user privacy: all personal information and the generated data from users are stored on the central servers of service providers, which is vulnerable to attacks and lead to data leakage, 3) un-guaranteed security: once any of those servers fails, user data stored in that server will be lost and cannot be recovered. 4) strong data isolation: data among multiple applications is difficult (if not impossible) to interact with each other, leading to extremely weak cross application interoperability.

To address the above problems, some emerging technologies are gradually attracting the attention of more and more researchers. Just to name a few, 1) Blockchain, which is a distributed ledger that combines data blocks in a sequential order, and is guaranteed to be non-tamperable and unforgeable equipped with cryptography. 2) Decentralized Identity, which is a globally unique, persistent and tamper proof personal identity, and it can be completely controlled by the owner and does not depend on the centralized platform and identity provider. 3) Distributed Storage, which is a scalable structure that uses distributed servers to share the storage and uses location servers to locate storage information, so that it can improve the reliability, availability, scalability of data systems.

Base on these rising technologies, we are trying to introduce some promising future research directions and some potential solutions, including but not limited to: cross-chain interaction, decentralized storage, multi-client multi-server transmission and security.

Along this line, the remainder of this paper is to first review the state-of-the-art network ecology, and then considers some of the rising technologies of Web3.0, at the developing stage of its conception, followed by some future directions.

2 The SOTA Network Ecology

2.1 Web Service

As the web has evolved, the nature of web services has become more apparent: it's about providing users with higher quality of experience through the use of new technologies. The existing Internet has motivated the rapid development of different areas in order to give users a higher quality of network services, especially in the area of storage and transmission. The essence of web services is to provide users with requested data efficiently. The quality of the user's network service is often reflected in the response time.

Web2.0 services store all content in centralized datacenters far away from users. Still, as the network grew, the number of users and data grew explosively, which inevitably burdened the data center and the network. Service or application providers often build or rent some suitable edge servers or edge nodes close to users to store a portion of frequently accessed contents in order to ensure faster delivery and reduce the redundant transmission of such contents, thus reducing the burden on data centers and networks. Latency can be reduced through proximity storage edge server, but with limited bandwidth resources and multiple transmission paths, there is a need to choose the right transmission path, whether it is at the edge server or edge node or to the data center, to get the data. This enables faster delivery of user-requested content to users and reduces possible network congestion, data loss, and other occurrences. The goal in the storage area is to reduce the back-to-source time by storing the content that users may access in the future through servers closer to the user's edge. In summary, the combination of storage and transport enables a higher quality of service for users in the current network.

2.2   Storage Architecture

Based on the development of edge computing, more edge servers can be fed to service or application providers, moving away from a single data center Web1.0. However, edge servers have limited storage resources and are widely distributed geographically. How to improve cache hit rate, transmission latency, etc., through cache replacement techniques, and deploy these edge servers for each application to reduce transmission latency has been a key research problem in industry and academia. Next, some representative cache replacement strategies and node deployment studies are briefly described.

The cache replacement strategy aims to ensure that the user's future requested content exists in the edge server as much as possible by real-time cache replacement within the limited storage space. To ensure that such content can be transferred to the user via edge servers close to the user instead of the more distant cloud in order to reduce the network transmission time. Traditional cache replacement strategies include LRU, LFU, and their variants [5], which are widely used in the industry due to their simplicity and ease of deployment. However, with the development of applications, these strategies lack performance in some specific scenarios, so intelligent cache replacement strategies [31,37,51,54] are proposed with popular content prediction based on artificial intelligence techniques. For example, Zhang et al. proposed GraphINF [54] as a popular content prediction strategy to obtain highly accurate hot content prediction results by exploiting the attractive geographical propagation characteristics of short videos, which supported the cache replacement strategy. Li et al. proposed the cache replacement strategy, CRATES [31], to solve the problem of low hit rate due to low-access frequency periods in short-video networks by predicting the possible future accessed popular content by exploiting the relationship between popular content and core users. Zhang et al. proposed distributed cache replacement strategy, AutoSight [53], to improve the caching hit rate by analyzing the popular periodicity and the unstable access characteristics in the short video network. And they designed an observation horizon for automatically acquiring popular content to prevent the ebb and flow of popular content from being unknown, thus reducing the obsolete content cached in the server.

The large number and wide distribution of edge servers are deployed as storage servers for service or application providers to store content. However, choosing which edge servers to use as storage servers is crucial because it directly affects the response time to user content requests and the cost to the provider. Data analysis revealed that some providers deploy many storage servers for services or applications to ensure lower response times. However, the frequency of requests from these servers is unbalanced, resulting in the wasting of storage resources and raising of the total cost. To avoid the unwelcome situation, a number of researchers have focused on the problem. For example, li et al. proposed edge storage nodes deployment strategy Frend [30], which presented a frequency-based transmission latency criterion by analyzing data and, using this criterion presented a deployment strategy that ensures both qualities of service and reduces the number of nodes.

Both the cache replacement strategy and the edge storage node deployment strategy have a role in improving the quality of user experience for Web2.0.

2.3 Transmission Mechanism

Based on decades-old network technologies and service architectures, Web1.0 placed limited requirements on network transmission. However, along with the developments of the network and the flourishing of services, Web2.0 put forward requirements on network transmission in terms of latency, bandwidth, packet loss rate, jitter, and more. To this end, some specialized technologies have been studied to optimize diversified services. Here, in this section, we introduce some classic works in network transmission optimization.

Multipath Transmission Control Protocol (MPTCP): Multi-home hosts are widespread, such as servers under Fat-tree network topology in the data center, or some smart devices with 5G/WIFI/Bluetooth multi-connectivity [26]. And such multi-home hosts will become more common with the deployment of IPv6. Traditional TCP can only exploit multiple connections by establishing multiple TCP connections since it only supports a single channel for an individual connection. To obtain the benefits of multi-connected network resources of the multi-home hosts, the proposed MPTCP supports the reverse multiplexing of redundant channels, which can increase the overall data transmission rate to the sum of all available channels [38]. Furthermore, in wireless network environments, MPTCP enables links to be added or dropped when clients enter or exit the network coverage, without breaking the end-to-end TCP connection. Thus, the problem of link switching can be solved at the endpoint instead of using any special handling mechanisms at the network or link level. Quick UDP Internet Connection (QUIC): The protocols of the transport layer mainly include TCP and User Datagram Protocol (UDP). The lightweight UDP is more efficient than TCP, which has been widely employed in many services, such as online games, streaming media, etc. But it is unable to provide reliable connections as TCP. To address the requirements of low connection latency and high reliability at the transport layer and application layer, Google proposed QUIC, a UDP-based protocol that incorporates the features of TCP, TLS, and HTTP/2

[25,29]. When the client connects to the server for the first time, QUIC only needs a delay of 1 Round Trip Time (RTT) to establish a reliable and secure connection, which is faster than 1–3 RTTs of TCP+TLS. After this connection, the client can cache the encrypted authentication information locally and establish a connection with the server again with 0 RTT connection establishment latency. As QUIC is based on UDP, it can reuse the multiplexing feature of the HTTP/2 protocol while avoiding the HTTP/2 Head-of-Line Blocking problem. Additionally, QUIC runs in the user space instead of the kernel space, which enables a fast update and deployment.

To meet the needs of Web2.0 where different services tend to prefer different performance paths, such as low latency, high bandwidth, low packet loss, etc., network layer protocols are not only limited to meet reachability but also ought to customize the routing paths for different types of flows. In this context, some learning-based routing algorithms have been proposed in recent years. For example, Cong et al. [13,15] proposed a multi-constraint reinforcement learning-based routing strategy by model fusion to provide different routing paths for different types of flows to fully utilize the available network resources; Zhang et al. [14] proposed a cross-domain routing decision mechanism assisted by intra-domain information based on homomorphic encryption technology, which can provide a good performance cross-domain routing path by leveraging intra-domain information.

3   Web3.0: Rising Technology

3.1   BlockChain

Blockchain technology emerged as the basis for crypto-currencies Bitcoin [36], has been widely applied to many frontiers with its characteristics of decentralization, tamper-resistant, traceability and anonymity. Blockchain is a chain of blocks that can be described as an immutable distributed database which records traceable transactions through cryptographic algorithms. It holds a shared distributed ledger without relying on a common trusted third party and is maintained by a group of nodes.

Depending on the degree of decentralization and openness, there are three types of blockchain: public blockchain, consortium blockchain and private blockchain. Public blockchains (also called permissionless blockchains) allow participants to access the network without any authentication. Two prominent examples are Bitcoin and Ethereum [9]. Consortium blockchains and private blockchains can be deemed permissioned blockchains where identity authentications are required when enrolling in the network. Permissioned blockchains are more common for organizations and enterprise demands and examples include Quorum [11], Corda [7], Hyperledger Fabric [4] and Tendermint [8].

Blockchains deploy smart contract to ensure ledger updating immutable and irreversible. Smart contract is a set of automated programms which are executed in virtual machines. It makes blockchains programmable and can be used to extend the state machines. For example, the Ethereum Virtual Machine (EVM) is used to store and execute smart contracts in Ethereum and for decentralized applications (DApps). Within smart contracts, blockchains can execute transactional workloads which have so far been handled almost exclusively by databases. Compared with traditional contract, smart contract executes itself without the involvement of third parties and uses cryptography to prevent random modifications of the ledger [6].

Traditional fault-tolerant consensus protocols have been adopted to blockchains for reaching a unified agreement on the state of the network in a decentralized way [10]. Normally the consensus needs a balance between resource consumption and security, since high degree of trust means high energy-intensive consensus. Bitcoin uses Proof-of-Work (PoW) as the consensus protocol. Mining nodes in Bitcoin compete on solving a cryptographic puzzle that is easy to verify to get the ledger writing right. Once a node finds the solution to the puzzle, it can propose a valid block and append it to the ledger. However, PoW consensus mechanism has some issues, for example, the 51% attack risk and large resource consumption. Ethereum2.0 changes from Proof-of-Work to Proof-of-Stake (PoS) and effectively improves the throughput. The new block is yield by validators who are elected according to the stake size or coin age, instead of miners. Compared with PoW, PoS consumes lower resource and is more robust to 51% attack. Recent blockchains like Tendermint and Hyperledger Fabric emphasize more on the security. Since there may be malicious nodes in the network, blockchain systems ought to be Byzantine fault-tolerant (BFT) [16]. They perform BFT state machine replication for deterministic state machines which supports up to one-third faulty replicas. PBFT is the first practical BFT protocol to work in an untrustworthy environment and tolerate Byzantine failures. PBFT consensus creates agreement on the global ledger state in the presence of Byzantine faults, while PoW and PoS only attain only crash fault-tolerant. However, since PBFT is a partially synchronous protocol, the value of the timer used to control the latency boundary is normally hard to set appropriately, which can then cause performance degradation.

3.2   Decentralized Identity

In most designs of Web3.0 network, a decentralized, verifiable and self-sovereign identity system is expected to be part of the Web3.0 infrastructure. Decentralized identity (DID), also called self-sovereign identity (SSI), is considered a key technology to realize the above requirements. In the traditional Internet, identity information is collected and handled by different big firms and organizations. An user cannot use the same social account on different platforms, which not only brings inconvenience to users, but also increases maintenance costs for web service providers. In addition, the right to disclose identity information is not controlled by users, thus there is a huge risk of user privacy leakage. The design goal of DID is to enable users to have full control over their identities, to use the same verifiable identity on different platforms, and to selectively expose or withhold their identity information.

So far, there have been some efforts to establish DID standards and design the specific implementation of DID. In the DID specification published by W3C [1], DIDs are defined as URIs that associate DID subjects with DID documents. DID documents provide cryptographic materials, verifiable methods and services for interaction with DID. In addition, W3C also defines verifiable credential (VC) [2], which is a machine-readable credential bound to a specific DID and provides a claim of a series of attributes associated with DID. A VC is issued by an entity called issuer to another entity called holder, and verified by entities called verifiers. For example, a university can issue a VC for the DID attributes about the degree the student has earned, and the student can hand over the VC to a company for proof when applying for a position. However, some definitions are still vague and need to be further specified in implementations. In implementation, DID is often closely related to distributed ledger technology, especially blockchain. Dunphy et al. [19] analyzed three representative DID platforms based on distributed ledgers at that time: Sovrin, uPort, and OneName. They believe that these platforms have defects such as dependence on centralized authorities, ad hoc trust and lack of usable user key management. Hyperledger Indy [3] is a DID implementation based on distributed ledgers. Indy Nodes jointly maintain a ledger in a decentralized manner to store identity records related to each DID. Organizations and individuals acquire the right to put transactions on the ledger by getting the role of Trust Anchor. CanDID, proposed by Maram et al. [34], solves the bootstrapping problem of existing standards and implementations by offering legacy-compatibility. It constructs user credentials and performs key recovery based on the user's existing web service account. It also offers more safety guarantees like sybil-resistance and accountability based on multiparty computation.

Based on the above works, we believe that any implementation of DID needs to have three important characteristics: decentralization, verifiability and privacy. However, there are still many trade-offs for DID to be widely used: How to ensure the authenticity and uniqueness of user registration while ensuring decentralization? How to ensure that malicious users can be audited while ensuring the privacy of other users? How to combine a DID system with existing blockchains and other distributed systems? These questions need to be further answered in future works.

3.3   Distributed Storage

Blockchains have been used as distributed storage system in many scenarios to achieve tamper-resistant storage, secure data access and robust data sharing. The features of traceability, immutability and auditability in blockchain are suitable for distributed data storage [33]. Authenticated data structure like Merkle Tree in the blockhead can be used to ensure the integrity of a query on the distributed ledger, which usually does not exist in the traditional database. Besides, fault-tolerant consensus protocol in blockchain detects potential misbehaviour and ensures the reliability of database operations without requiring the involvement of a central trusted party. BigchainDB [35] is the first decentralized database system based on blockchain which leverages some effective blockchain features to construct a shared database in a distrusting environment while avoiding the drawbacks brought from blockchain. FalconDB [39] proposed a blockchain-based database which provides verifiable and integral query results and prevents undesired operations through incentive mechanism.

Fusion between distributed storage system and blockchains is an upward trend since it is possible to apply techniques in traditional distributed database to the blockchain. For example, an significant storage scalability issue in blockchain originates from the full-replication data storage scheme, that is, a full node maintains a record of the whole block data of the ledger. BFT-store [41] utilizes the storage partition approach which is adopted in distributed storage system scale out blockchain. It uses erasure coding to divide a block into several chunks and assign these chunks to each node together with some parties for storage. Fan et al. [20] proposed a group storage mechanism which allows multiple nodes jointly maintain a complete copy of the ledger to reduce per-node storage overhead. Distributed database applies crash fault-tolerant consensus protocol like Raft for state replication while blockchains can use Byzantine fault-tolerant protocol like PBFT to prevent malicious operations. However, it improves security at the expense of performance. Concurrency control techniques adopted in the distributed database system are being used to enhance the performance of blockchains [44]. Hyperledger Fabric supports concurrent transaction execution and uses optimistic concurrency control to improve parallelism. Moreover, sharding has been proved to be an effective way to improve scalability while maintain high security [18]. Examples of recent sharded blockchains include Brokerchain [24], Pyramid [23] and Monoxide [47]. By leveraging sharding protocols in traditional distributed system as a technique to reduce cost of consensus protocols, the transactional throughput increases at scale.

4   Future Directions

4.1   Cross-Chain Technology

Cross-chain technology, also called blockchain interoperability, refers to protocols or platforms that enable homogeneous or heterogeneous blockchains to communicate with each other in a verifiable manner. While there have been many different blockchain platforms aim to serve Web3.0, the lack of a unified cross-chain scheme hinders these platforms from working together as a generic Web3.0 infrastructure. Due to the heterogeneity of existing blockchain platforms, including differences in consensus algorithms, smart contract languages, and access rights, these platforms cannot interoperate through a unified protocol or interface, thus becoming data silos in the Web3.0 world. Liu et al. [32] proposed that a secure interoperability platform is one of the three key enablers of Web 3.0 (the other two are independent blockchains and federated or centralized platforms that provide verifiable states for blockchains). As cross-chain has become an increasingly concerning research topic in both Web3.0 and blockchain scalability, some existing works have tried to design cross-chain platforms or protocols from different aspects. In this section, we try to analyze the characteristics and shortcomings of some representative works, and finally propose a possible cross-chain framework.

Cross-chain communication first appeared between homogeneous blockchains to improve the scalability of the overall system. Sidechain is one of the earliest cross-chain technologies. It mainly refers to the expansion of public blockchains, such as Bitcoin and Ethereum, in the form of another chain [21]. Asset transfer is carried out between the main chain and the sidechain through a certain protocol, a representative example of which is a two-way peg [45]. When a portion of the asset is to be transferred from the main chain to the side chain, a certain amount of tokens on the main chain needs to be sent to a special address and then locked, and tokens of the same value are created on the side chain. This method improves the overall scalability of blockchain without affecting the performance of the main chain, but the application is limited to the asset exchange of homogeneous blockchains. A more general form of cross-chain than sidechains is the cross-shard protocol. Sharding, as one of the most commonly used horizontal expansion methods in traditional distributed systems, is also used by some blockchains to improve their scalability [18,27,50]. Transactions between different shards, i.e. homogeneous blockchains, are carried out in the form of cross-shard transactions. Existing cross-shard protocols usually focus on the safety and atomicity of cross-shard transactions. For example, Omniledger [27] relies on clients to assist with cross-shard transactions. RapidChain [50] splits a cross-shard transaction into multiple intra-shard transactions based on the UTXO model. AHL [18] designs a 2PC and 2PL protocol based on a reference committee to guarantee atomicity and isolation. Although the application scope of the cross-shard protocols has expanded from token exchange to more general transactions compared to sidechains, it can only achieve communication between homogeneous blockchains, which is not sufficient to meet the requirements of Web3.0.

Cross-chain communication between heterogeneous blockchains is another issue for interoperations. Relay technology is one solution by constructing another chain or a relay structure between two chains to verify the validity of the cross-chain transactions and forward them from one chain to the other. Examples include Cosmos [28], and Polkadot [49] solve cross-chain issues by using the Cosmos Hub or Polkadot Relay Chain to provide interconnections. However, the above two solutions has poor security guarantee and fail to consider the active status of nodes, which is not conducive to the efficient execution of the system. He et al. [22] proposed a nested blockchain architecture and dynamically select the high efficient nodes to construct the relay chain for stable and low-latency cross-chain communication. Hashed time-locks is implemented through the Hashed TimeLock Contract (HTLC) [48] to build a bidirectional payment channel within a certain period of time. The lightning network [40] is a typical hashed time-locks project fund on top of the Bitcoin. It has an assumption that the amount of the single payment is small enough. It ensures a small loss of one party in the transaction even if one party defaults. Hashed time-locks allows atomic swap between heterogeneous blockchains which means the valid cross-chain transactions must be executed simultaneously on both chains. Moreover, it usually supports only micro-payments and the atomic swap may lead to high waiting time, which limits its use in large-scale applications. The Notary mechanism [42] uses a third party to propose transactions and exchange data between two chains which does not require the authentication of transaction participants' identity. It is a more reasonable and secure approach since the system security is enhanced when some nodes are injected by malicious one or crash errors occur. However, it may involve unverified nodes operating in a dishonest manner, since the identity verification during cross-chain communication is critical for making blockchains interoperable.

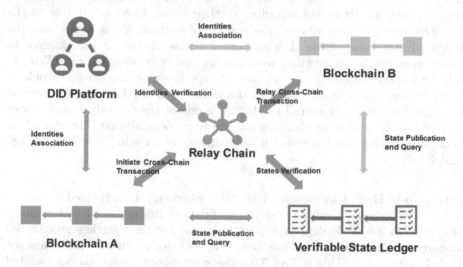

Fig. 1. A general cross-chain framework abstraction

Based on the above works, we propose a simple but universal cross-chain framework design, as shown in Fig. 1. We believe that a general cross-chain framework requires three key pieces of information: global user identities, the ledger states of different blockchains, and the network and service information of different blockchains. Therefore our proposed framework consists of the following three components: a DID platform, a verifiable state ledger, and a relay chain. The DID platform provides global verifiable identity credentials, and each user associates their identities registered in different chains with their DID. Different blockchains register state information that requires external verification in the cross-chain process on the verifiable state ledger. For example, a consortium blockchain member can publish the content and signature of a specific block that is otherwise inaccessible to the outside world through the verifiable ledger. The relay chain is responsible for registering the network addresses and service interfaces of different blockchains, forwarding transactions to different blockchains and verifying cross-chain transactions with the help of the DID platform and verifiable state ledger. Here we do not specify the implementation forms of these three components, but we recommend adopting blockchain using hybrid consensus to ensure performance and decentralization at the same time. In addition, each component can be implemented on the same blockchain together with other components, or a component can be composed of multiple blockchains. We leave more specific implementation details to future works, and hope this cross-chain framework abstraction can be helpful to researchers in this field.

4.2   AI-Based Caching and Storaging

In Web 2.0, due to the centralization of data storage, it is only necessary to store the content attributes according to their value. In Web 3.0, due to the decentralization of data storage, the storage of content across nodes, and the unique identification of user IDs and other characteristics, it has changed to mainly measure the value of user attributes for storage. Compared with Web 2.0, web 3.0 storage considerations are more complex, so solving storage problems under challenging situations through the advantages of AI technology may be a potential solution. Decentralized storage is one of the critical technologies of web 3.0, which faces many challenges in future implementation. Therefore, how to improve the hit rate is a research focus of node storage in the web3.0 storage model.

Cross-Node Data Placement. Web 3.0 is inherently decentralized in content storage and does not require the creation of data center nodes for each application. So Web 3.0 rarely deploys applications that run on a single server (node) or store data in a single database. But, this does not mean that nodes are not needed to store data. That is, Web 3.0 nodes store mixed types of data associated with users from various applications, i.e., data generated by the same application need to be placed across nodes based on user attributes. Therefore, placing the user-requested data across nodes by selecting appropriate nodes among many nodes ensures low response time and high space utilization of stored content.

User Request Content Retrieval. The data is placed across nodes, which means that not only a few or even one service or application's data is stored in each server node. This also means that each service or application may occupy all the available storage servers to store the data. Additionally, due to the vast amount of requested data, how to retrieve the requested content and efficiently find the storage location where cache the requested content is one of the potential future research directions.

Hit Rate Improvement of Storage Node. In order to ensure the quality of user experience, it is theoretically necessary to store the user's future requested content on the storage nodes closer to the user to reduce the response time. Although the total number of nodes is large, the number of nodes adjacent to users is smaller than the number of users. Additionally, the edge server storage space is limited, so storing the content of all users required through adjacent nodes is difficult. So it is impossible to place the content of future user requests in the neighboring nodes. Furthermore, because of the variety of applications and the vast amount of data content, it is impossible to know which content will be requested by the user in the future. If the stored content is not what the user will access in the future, this will seriously affect the quality of the user's experience. Therefore, how to improve the hit rate that the content stored in nodes is the content requested by users in the future is a research focus of node storage in the web3.0 storage model.

Availability Guarantee of Storage Content. In daily use, the storage node is unavailable due to the aging of the equipment and other irresistible factors, which affects the use of the data stored on the node. When the node is out of the network, how to ensure that the data inside the unavailable node is still available is an inevitable future research direction.

4.3 Web 3.0 Transmission

Compared with the centralized features of web 2.0, web 3.0 aims to establish a user-owned and user-constructed decentralized network ecology. Accordingly, web 3.0 architecture has two main characteristics: content-driven addressing and multi-client and multi-server transmission. Hence, for these two features, we analyze the challenges and propose potential solutions in transmission perspective in this paper.

Content Driven Addressing. In contrast to existing network architecture, a key feature of web 3.0 transmissions is content-driven. Given the developments from IPv4 to IPv6, incremental deployment is particularly important in the network architecture evolution. Hence, we propose an incrementally deployable content-based addressing architecture.

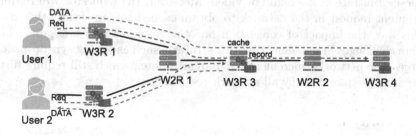

Fig. 2. Incrementally deployable content-based addressing architecture

As shown in the Fig. 2, suppose there are two types of routers, one is the traditional router that supports IP traffic, called $W2R$ for convenience, and the other is the content-based addressing-enabled router for web 3.0, called $W3R$. When $User_1$ sends a content request, $W3R_1$ converts the content-based request message into an IP-based packet, where the content index is converted into an IP address and forwarded to $W2R_1$. In this paper, we do not discuss specific techniques of conversion. A strawman way is mapping, whose corresponding massive mapping entries can be mitigated by [12,52]. $W2R_1$ forwards the IP-based content request to $W3R_3$ as per the operation of IP traffic; likewise, the request will be eventually forwarded to $W3R_4$. Assuming that $W3R_4$ can provide the requested contents, then it can deliver the data based on the information in the packet header back to $User_1$. $W3R_3$ will cache the corresponding content when transmitting it in response to the same content requests. When $User_2$ proposes the same content request, the cached of the last request of $User_1$ will be delivered back by $W3R_3$ directly.

Multi-clients and Multi-servers Transmission. In web 3.0, all nodes can act as content producers, and there exists the demand to integrate content from multiple parties, i.e., a content request may need multi-users to respond. However, when multiple parties send back the required data at a short interval will lead to network congestion or even packet loss. Moreover, it is common that multiple requestors to request the same popular content, i.e., the transmission between multiple clients and multiple servers (MCMS) situation, which can aggravate such issues. In this paper, we propose a traffic control strategy for this potential MCMS situation.

Some existing traffic control in network transmission of web2.0 is usually conducted by the sender, which determines whether there are congestion based on some congestion control signals or timestamp information, and then executes corresponding traffic control actions. Based on this, we propose a request-side assisted traffic control strategy. When the congestion ratio of multiple response traffics of a request reaches α (the probability of the congestion caused by this requestor is positively correlated with α), then the requestor will reduce the demand with a probability of $\beta\alpha$ (where $\beta \in [0, 1]$), such as requestor reduces the desired bitrate of the audio or video. Moreover, the requestor will re-diffuse the content request in the network to obtain cached content from other nodes. In this way, the impact of congestion on other users can be mitigated. There still are challenges in implementing this strategy, such as timing synchronization of large-scale networks, incremental deployment, etc., which still require further research and exploration by all network researchers.

4.4   Security Issues

Compared with Web2.0, where user data is stored and controlled by service providers to optimize the user's experience on the Internet. The basic goal of Web3.0 is for users to control and manage their own data, and service provider need to apply users for data use, thus more attention is paid to user privacy protection in Web3.0. Therefore, compared with the traditional security protection on the server side, the client side and the data transmission, Web3.0 has stricter security requirements.

Security on the User Side. In Web3.0, personal digital assets are completely owned and controlled by individuals, and the server no longer has backup of user data. This makes users take on a greater responsibility for their data than in the Web2.0 era, which also means that users are more vulnerable to attacks and may suffer greater losses when attacked. For example, the rapidly developing Crypto Wallet [46], NFT, etc. have great real value (which can be converted into real currency), so they are more frequently attacked by hackers such as private key theft, airdrop scams(NFT) and authorization attacks. Moreover, Whether Web3.0 data will be accepted by other user is also a question while the cyberspace is an untrustworthy environment and the peer identity should be verified. The Web3.0 service provider and user must making a choice about who and how to make the authentication.

Security in Transmission. Web3.0's emphasis on privacy makes privacy protection algorithms more important. In the Web2.0 system, it's more necessary to protect the user's data from being known by third parties other than the server and the user during the transmission process. In Web3.0, there is also user identity information that needs to be protected to help users "incognito". One solution is Mixnet [43], which is a decentralized network arranged in a multi-layered format. The user converts the message packets into encrypted "Sphinx" [17] packets instead of sending messages directly over the Internet and the "Sphinx" packets are untraceable, and then shuffles through the Mixnode (mixed network).

Security on the Server Side. The problems on the server side are caused by the design and technology of the Web3.0 system. Even though blockchain is one of the most secure technologies, hackers may get unauthorized access to wallets and other digital assets by exploiting cryptography flaws. And if the breach occurs, it is nearly hard to recover the lost funds or digital assets. Moreover, there is no way to track completed transactions and retrieve lost money. This makes it necessary to provide an effective response at the system fundamental level to assure users of the safety and security of their data and information. Key management is the basis for users to conduct transactions in Web3.0, but at the same time key management is also a very difficult problem. This drives users to choose custodial wallet over non-custodial wallet. However, custodial wallet will lead to the creation of a kind of centralized management wallet application, which is contrary to the fully decentralized direction of Web3.0.

Data decentralization and anonymity are the cornerstones and advantages of Web3.0, but while strengthening user's data privacy also mean that it's difficult to be regulated by the government. Cause Web3.0 to become the platform of many illegal crimes, which has brought great limitations to large-scale promotion of blockchain and Web3.0. In conclusion, before solving the above problems, there is still a long way to go and a lot of content that needs continuous research.

5   Conclusion

Web3.0 is a fully open and decentralized Internet which allows each user to control their data, but there still exist some technical challenges. This papers first introduce the current network architecture, and then analyze several key technologies of web3.0 network, including cross-chain interaction, web3.0 storage, web3.0 transmission and security issues, which we believe will provide reference for relevant researches.

References

1. W3C: Decentralized Identifiers (DIDs) v1.0. https://www.w3.org/TR/did-core/. Accessed 15 Oct 2022
2. W3C: Decentralized Identifiers (DIDs) v1.0. https://www.w3.org/TR/vc-data-model/. Accessed 15 Oct 2022
3. Hyperledger Indy. https://www.hyperledger.org/use/hyperledger-indy/. Accessed 15 Oct 2022
4. Androulaki, E., et al.: Hyperledger fabric: a distributed operating system for permissioned blockchains. In: Proceedings of the Thirteenth EuroSys Conference, pp. 1–15 (2018)
5. Arlitt, M.F., Cherkasova, L., Dilley, J., Friedrich, R., Jin, T.: Evaluating content management techniques for web proxy caches. SIGMETRICS Perform. Eval. Rev. **27**(4), 3–11 (2000). https://doi.org/10.1145/346000.346003
6. Atzei, N., Bartoletti, M., Cimoli, T.: A survey of attacks on ethereum smart contracts (SoK). In: Maffei, M., Ryan, M. (eds.) POST 2017. LNCS, vol. 10204, pp. 164–186. Springer, Heidelberg (2017). https://doi.org/10.1007/978-3-662-54455-6_8
7. Brown, R.G.: The corda platform: an introduction. Retrieved 27, 2018 (2018)
8. Buchman, E.: Tendermint: byzantine fault tolerance in the age of blockchains. Ph.D. thesis, University of Guelph (2016)
9. Buterin, V., et al.: A next-generation smart contract and decentralized application platform. In: White paper, vol. 3, no. 37, p. 2-1 (2014)
10. Cachin, C., et al.: Blockchains and consensus protocols. The Wild (2017)
11. Chase, J.M.: Quorum White paper (2016). Accessed 17 Jan 2019
12. Cong, P., Zhang, Y., Liu, B., Wang, W., Xiong, Z., Xu, K.: A&b: AI and block-based TCAM entries replacement scheme for routers. IEEE J. Sel. Areas Commun. **40**(9), 2643–2661 (2022)
13. Cong, P., et al.: A deep reinforcement learning-based multi-optimality routing scheme for dynamic IoT networks. Comput. Netw. **192**, 108057 (2021)
14. Cong, P., et al.: Break the blackbox! Desensitize intra-domain information for inter-domain routing. In: 2022 IEEE/ACM 30th International Symposium on Quality of Service (IWQoS), pp. 1–10. IEEE (2022)

15. Cong, P., Zhang, Y., Wang, W., Xu, K., Li, R., Li, F.: A deep reinforcement learning-based routing scheme with two modes for dynamic networks. In: ICC 2021-IEEE International Conference on Communications, pp. 1–6. IEEE (2021)
16. Correia, M.: From byzantine consensus to blockchain consensus. In: Essentials of Blockchain Technology, pp. 41–80. Chapman and Hall/CRC, Hoboken (2019)
17. Danezis, G., Goldberg, I.: Sphinx: a compact and provably secure mix format. In: 2009 30th IEEE Symposium on Security and Privacy, pp. 269–282 (2009)
18. Dang, H., Dinh, T.T.A., Loghin, D., Chang, E.C., Lin, Q., Ooi, B.C.: Towards scaling blockchain systems via sharding. In: Proceedings of the 2019 international conference on management of data, pp. 123–140 (2019)
19. Dunphy, P., Petitcolas, F.A.: A first look at identity management schemes on the blockchain. IEEE Secur. Priv. **16**(4), 20–29 (2018)
20. Fan, Y., et al.: DLBN: Group storage mechanism based on double layer blockchain network. IEEE Internet Things J. (2022)
21. Gaži, P., Kiayias, A., Zindros, D.: Proof-of-stake sidechains. In: 2019 IEEE Symposium on Security and Privacy (SP), pp. 139–156. IEEE (2019)
22. He, X., Zhang, Y., Wang, X.: A scalable nested blockchain framework with dynamic node selection approach for IoT. In: 2022 IEEE International Performance, Computing, and Communications Conference (IPCCC), pp. 108–113. IEEE (2022)
23. Hong, Z., Guo, S., Li, P., Chen, W.: Pyramid: a layered sharding blockchain system. In: IEEE INFOCOM 2021-IEEE Conference on Computer Communications, pp. 1–10. IEEE (2021)
24. Huang, H., et al.: Brokerchain: a cross-shard blockchain protocol for account/balance-based state sharding. In: IEEE INFOCOM (2022)
25. Kakhki, A.M., Jero, S., Choffnes, D., Nita-Rotaru, C., Mislove, A.: Taking a long look at QUIC: an approach for rigorous evaluation of rapidly evolving transport protocols. In: Proceedings of the 2017 Internet Measurement Conference, pp. 290–303 (2017)
26. Khalili, R., Gast, N., Popovic, M., Le Boudec, J.Y.: MPTCP is not pareto-optimal: performance issues and a possible solution. IEEE/ACM Trans. Network. **21**(5), 1651–1665 (2013)
27. Kokoris-Kogias, E., Jovanovic, P., Gasser, L., Gailly, N., Syta, E., Ford, B.: Omniledger: a secure, scale-out, decentralized ledger via sharding. In: 2018 IEEE Symposium on Security and Privacy (SP), pp. 583–598. IEEE (2018)
28. Kwon, J., Buchman, E.: Cosmos Whitepaper. A Netw. Distrib. Ledgers (2019)
29. Langley, A., Riddoch, A., Wilk, A., et al.: The QUIC transport protocol: design and internet-scale deployment. In: Proceedings of the Conference of the ACM Special Interest Group on Data Communication, pp. 183–196 (2017)
30. Li, P., et al.: Frend for edge servers: reduce server number! Keeping service quality! In: 2021 IEEE 23rd International Conference on High Performance Computing and Communications; 7th International Conference on Data Science and Systems; 19th International Conference on Smart City; 7th International Conference on Dependability in Sensor, Cloud and Big Data Systems and Application (HPCC/DSS/SmartCity/DependSys), Haikou, Hainan, China, 20–22, December 2021, pp. 107–114. IEEE (2021)
31. Li, P., Zhang, Y., Zhang, H., Wang, W., Xu, K., Zhang, Z.: CRATES: a cache replacement algorithm for low access frequency period in edge server. In: 17th International Conference on Mobility, Sensing and Networking, MSN 2021, Exeter, United Kingdom, 13–15 December 2021, pp. 128–135. IEEE (2021), https://doi.org/10.1109/MSN53354.2021.00033

32. Liu, Z., et al.: Make web3. 0 connected. IEEE Trans. Depend. Secure Comput. (2021)
33. Maiyya, S., Zakhary, V., Amiri, M.J., Agrawal, D., El Abbadi, A.: Database and distributed computing foundations of blockchains. In: Proceedings of the 2019 International Conference on Management of Data, pp. 2036–2041 (2019)
34. Maram, D., et al.: Candid: can-do decentralized identity with legacy compatibility, sybil-resistance, and accountability. In: 2021 IEEE Symposium on Security and Privacy (SP), pp. 1348–1366. IEEE (2021)
35. McConaghy, T., et al.: Bigchaindb: a scalable blockchain database. White paper, BigChainDB (2016)
36. Nakamoto, S.: Bitcoin: a peer-to-peer electronic cash system. Decentralized Bus. Rev. 21260 (2008)
37. Narayanan, A., Verma, S., Ramadan, E., Babaie, P., Zhang, Z.L.: Deepcache: a deep learning based framework for content caching. In: Proceedings of the 2018 Workshop on Network Meets AI and ML, pp. 48–53. ACM (2018)
38. Nishida, Y., Eardley, P.: MPTCP-multipath TCP. In: WG Meeting, vol. 5 (2011)
39. Peng, Y., Du, M., Li, F., Cheng, R., Song, D.: FalconDB: blockchain-based collaborative database. In: Proceedings of the 2020 ACM SIGMOD International Conference on Management of Data, pp. 637–652 (2020)
40. Poon, J., Dryja, T.: The bitcoin lightning network: scalable off-chain instant payments (2016)
41. Qi, X., Zhang, Z., Jin, C., Zhou, A.: BFT-store: storage partition for permissioned blockchain via erasure coding. In: 2020 IEEE 36th International Conference on Data Engineering (ICDE), pp. 1926–1929. IEEE (2020)
42. Qin, K., Gervais, A.: An overview of blockchain scalability, interoperability and sustainability. Hochschule Luzern Imperial College London Liquidity Network (2018)
43. Sampigethaya, K., Poovendran, R.: A survey on mix networks and their secure applications. Proc. IEEE 94(12), 2142–2181 (2006)
44. Sharma, A., Schuhknecht, F.M., Agrawal, D., Dittrich, J.: Blurring the lines between blockchains and database systems: the case of hyperledger fabric. In: Proceedings of the 2019 International Conference on Management of Data, pp. 105–122 (2019)
45. Singh, A., Click, K., Parizi, R.M., Zhang, Q., Dehghantanha, A., Choo, K.K.R.: Sidechain technologies in blockchain networks: an examination and state-of-the-art review. J. Netw. Comput. Appl. 149, 102471 (2020)
46. Suratkar, S., Shirole, M., Bhirud, S.: Cryptocurrency wallet: a review. In: 2020 4th International Conference on Computer, Communication and Signal Processing (ICCCSP), pp. 1–7 (2020)
47. Wang, J., Wang, H.: Monoxide: scale out blockchains with asynchronous consensus zones. In: 16th USENIX Symposium on Networked Systems Design and Implementation (NSDI 2019), pp. 95–112 (2019)
48. Wiki, B.: Hash Time Locked Contracts (2016)
49. Wood, G.: Polkadot: vision for a heterogeneous multi-chain framework. In: White paper, vol. 21, pp. 2327–4662 (2016)
50. Zamani, M., Movahedi, M., Raykova, M.: Rapidchain: scaling blockchain via full sharding. In: Proceedings of the 2018 ACM SIGSAC Conference on Computer and Communications Security, pp. 931–948 (2018)
51. Zhang, X., Qi, Z., Min, G., Miao, W., Fan, Q., Ma, Z.: Cooperative edge caching based on temporal convolutional networks. IEEE Trans. Parallel Distrib. Syst. 33(9), 2093–2105 (2022). https://doi.org/10.1109/TPDS.2021.3135257

52. Zhang, Y., Cong, P., Liu, B., Wang, W., Xu, K.: Air: An AI-based TCAM entry replacement scheme for routers. In: 2021 IEEE/ACM 29th International Symposium on Quality of Service (IWQOS), pp. 1–10. IEEE (2021)
53. Zhang, Y., et al.: Autosight: distributed edge caching in short video network. IEEE Netw. **34**(3), 194–199 (2020). https://doi.org/10.1109/MNET.001.1900345
54. Zhang, Y.: GraphInf: a GCN-based popularity prediction system for short video networks. In: Ku, W.-S., Kanemasa, Y., Serhani, M.A., Zhang, L.-J. (eds.) ICWS 2020. LNCS, vol. 12406, pp. 61–76. Springer, Cham (2020). https://doi.org/10. 1007/978-3-030-59618-7_5

A Hybrid Recommendation Model for Social Network Services Using Twitter Data

Ping Han[1,2], Jingwei Hong[1,3], Abdur Rasool[1,2]([⊠]), Hui Chen[4,5],
Yi Pan[1], and Qingshan Jiang[1]([⊠])

[1] Shenzhen Institute of Advanced Technology, Chinese Academy of Sciences,
Shenzhen 518055, China
{rasool,qs.jiang}@siat.ac.cn
[2] Shenzhen College of Advanced Technology,
University of Chinese Academy of Sciences, Beijing 100049, China
[3] College of Mathematics and Information Science, Hebei University,
Baoding 071002, China
[4] Shenzhen Polytechnic, Shenzhen 518055, Guangdong, China
[5] Institute of Applied Mathematics, Hebei Academy of Science, Hebei 050081, China

Abstract. With the continuous popularization of social networking sites, e.g., Twitter and Facebook, people's requirements for the quality of social network services are rising rapidly. Traditional personalized recommendation models rely on independent algorithms, i.e., streaming ranking algorithms, content-based algorithms, and collaborative filtering analysis. However, the recommendation performance of these models for different users is not stable, resulting in poor user experience on such web services. To tackle this issue, we propose a novel recommendation model integrating multiple recommendation algorithms, which can make corresponding recommendations according to the characteristics of users. The comparative analysis with Twitter data shows that the proposed model performs better than the traditional models.

Keywords: Social networking services · Web user experience · User recommendation · Twitter data

1 Introduction

In recent years, the development of online social networks has boosted various mobile social applications such as Facebook and Twitter, which have deeply affected people's lives. People can use social platforms to communicate with each other and share user information to obtain their desired information and follow the person they are interested in [1]. For example, Twitter is one of the

Supported by The National Key Research and Development Program of China under Grant No. 2021YFF1200104, and Hebei Academy of Sciences under Grant No. 22602.

most popular social networks. It has 650 million registered users and is the third most popular after Instagram and Facebook. Twitter has 152 million daily active users and accommodates 500 million daily tweets [2].

People usually establish network contacts on social platforms with people who are familiar with each other or have similar interests. However, due to a large number of social media users, it is not easy to find people to contact, which reduces the effectiveness of the network for users [3]. To a certain extent, the level of intelligent recommendation service determines people's satisfaction with their spiritual life [4]. At present, the research on intelligent recommendation algorithms has been pervasive. The performance of the recommendation system is affected by its recommendation algorithm. Traditional personalized recommendation systems can be divided into influential ranking algorithms, content-based algorithms, and collaborative filtering analysis [5].

In the research field of social networks, influential user ranking is a hot topic. In reality, many applications related to social networks depend on the influence ranking of network nodes/users. Information from the accounts of the most influential public celebrities can quickly spread to the entire network, so identifying influential users is of great significance in recommendation algorithms [6]. The widely used network node ranking algorithm in recent years is PageRank. The most famous example is Google's search engine, which ranks search results according to the importance of the pages associated with keywords. In view of the structural similarity between Twitter and www, we can apply the PageRank algorithm to the Twitter network [7].

The contend-based recommendation algorithm or model obtains users' interests through user-generated content and recommends items with similar content to users [8]. Collaborative filtering is the most common recommendation algorithm proposed by Goldberg. The idea is to calculate the neighbor user list based on the score matrix, predict the user's favorite items, and recommend the items with high scores to users [9]. Collaborative filtering recommendation methods mainly include user-based recommendation methods and project-based recommendation methods. The user-based method first finds a group of people with the same interests as the target users and then recommends the projects they like. In contrast, the project-based method first calculates the similarity between projects through the user's behavior and then recommends the most similar project that the target user likes [10].

These recommendation models do not consider the difference in user characteristics, and the recommendation performance for different users is unstable. For example, the content-based model recommends unknown people to users, while social graph-based methods tend to recommend known people to users [11]. To solve these problems, we propose a new model that is based on a hybrid recommendation system that integrates multiple recommendation algorithms to improve the recommendation performance. This model (IIRM) effectively recommended the influential user over the social network web services by analyzing the hit ratio. We experimented with Twitter data to evaluate the hit ratio by our proposed model, HRM. Hence, there are two following significant contributions.

- A new hybrid recommendation model (HRM) is proposed that integrates multiple recommendation algorithms to improve the social network's recommendation performance.
- This model (HRM) effectively recommended the influential user over the social network web services by analyzing the hit ratio of Twitter data.

This study can be applied to marketing and shopping websites that deal with thousands of active users globally. This model can help them to identify influential users for their products.

2   Proposed Methodology

2.1   PageRank

The numerical weight that it assigns to any given element E is referred to as the PageRank of E and is denoted by $PR(E)$. $PR(A)$ is calculated by the following formula [12].

$$PR(A) = 1 - d + \left(\frac{PR(B)}{L(B)} + \frac{PR(C)}{L(C)} + \frac{PR(D)}{L(D)} + \cdots \right) \qquad (1)$$

where L is the number of outbound links, and d is a damping factor which is set as 0.85. However, the other training parameters have been randomly selected.

2.2   Mutual Follower

The concept of the mutual follower was previously defined in [13]. This study assumes that the more followers a candidate has, the more important he is. As shown in Fig. 1, the arrow pointing from a to b means a follows b.

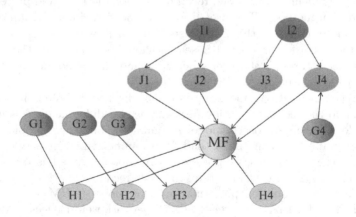

Fig. 1. Interaction of mutual followers with different candidates.

The number of mutual followers (MF) is defined as Eq. 2, where u and c indicate user and a candidate, respectively.

$$MF(u,c) = | \{ \text{ user } a \mid F(u,a) \text{ and } F(a,c) \text{ and } UF(u,c) \} | \qquad (2)$$

where $u \neq a \neq c$, which means a user u follows a user a, the user a follows a user c and the user u doesn't follow the user c, then the user u is one mutual follower of the user c.

2.3 Profile Matching

Profile matching is implemented by using the time zone information of the user profile because it has been used traditionally and effectively to calculate geographical proximity. If the same time zone is found in the configuration files of two users, u and c, the $PM(u,c)$ function returns 1; otherwise, it returns 0 [14].

2.4 Hybrid Recommendation Model (HRM)

A recommendation hit is an event where an active user follows a suggested person by the algorithm. We define Recommendation Hit Ratio (RHR) as the number of Recommendation Hit (RH) to the number of actual people followed by the active user (AU), where an algorithm RA_k is applied to a user u [15].

$$RHR(RA_k(u)) = \frac{RH(RA_k(u))}{AU(u)} \qquad (3)$$

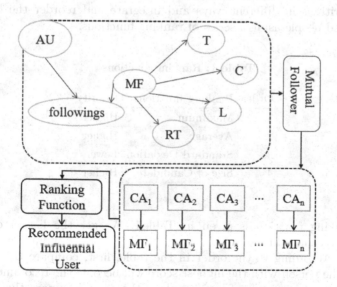

Fig. 2. The procedures of HRM algorithms.

Recommendation Precision (RP) refers to how accurately an algorithm suggests candidates to an active user. The recommendation score (RS) is calculated by the position of a hit candidate in the list, and we defined it as the ratio of the average of all hit candidates (c_{hit}) to candidate list size.

$$RP(u) = \left(1 - \frac{\text{MEAN}\left(RS_{RA_k}\left(c_{hit}\right)\right)}{L\left(RA_k(u)\right)}\right) \times 100 \tag{4}$$

where L is the size of the candidates' list generated by RA_k.

$$\text{MEAN}\left(RS_{RA_k}\left(c_{hit}\right)\right) = \frac{\sum_{i=1}^{h} RS_{RA_k}\left(c_i\right)}{h} \tag{5}$$

where h is the number of recommendation hits. The structure of the proposed algorithm is illustrated in Fig. 2.

We also introduce a comprehensive standard, coefficient of variation(CV), as defined above. If MEAN increases while STDDEV decreases, then CV decreases, and vice versa. Thus, we can choose a method with lower CV.

$$\text{CV(m)} = \frac{\text{STDDEV(m)}}{\text{MEAN(m)}} \tag{6}$$

where m is either RHR or RP.

To train the model, firstly, we generate a user feature pool consisting of a local social graph of an active user (AU). Mutual follower (MF) is in the list of recommended people, which has features, e.g., comments (C), likes (L), retweets (RT), and tweets (T). Secondly, we apply the different single recommendation algorithms to get the initial candidate list. Then, we combine these recommendation algorithms in different ways and integrate and reorder the list of the recommended people using a series of ranking functions.

Table 1. Ranking functions.

Order	Ranking functions	Priority
1	Maximum	Higher
2	Average	Higher
3	Standard Deviation	Lower
4	Size of Candidate	Higher

The ranking function is given in Table 1. We get the list of candidates with single recommendation algorithms and their corresponding recommendation scores. According to the order in the table, first, compare the maximum score, and the person with the highest score will become the recommended person. If the maximum score of two people is the same, compare the average of the two, and so on, to get the final candidate.

3   Experiment Evaluation

To evaluate the performance of our proposed model, we used the Open Twitter dataset [16] to test and compare the hit ratio of several recommendation algorithms. The recommendation hit ratio and the precision contrast between the Double, Triple, and Quadruple algorithms and the HRM model are compared.

Table 2. The combinations types of different recommendation algorithms.

Combination type	recommendation algorithms
Single	PageRank (pr), Mutual follower (mf), Number of tweets (nt), Profile matching (pm), Number of followers (nf)
Proposed HRM (double)	prmf, prnt, pmmf, prpm, nfmf, nfpm
Proposed HRM (triple)	prmfnt, prmfnf, pmmfnf
Proposed HRM (quad)	prmfntnf, prpmmfnf

As shown in Table 2, we use some combination of five recommendation algorithms to apply to our proposed model; then we select the 100 users who most follow others from the dataset, compare the performance of these combined algorithms in the recommendation hit ratio (representing the proportion of users recommended by the algorithm which are actually followed by these 100 users.)

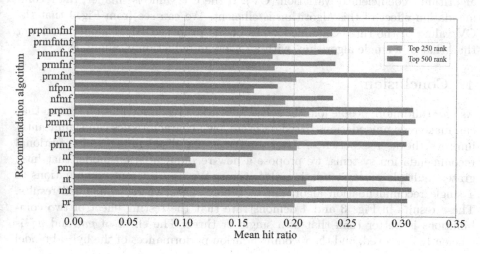

Fig. 0. Mean hit ratio of top 250 & top 500 by used recommendation algorithms.

Figure 3 shows each combination algorithm's recommendation hit ratio calculation results (use the real following of the 100 users divided by the rankings of the top 250 and 500 users generated by each algorithm). Compared with single algorithms, we can see that all HRM model (Double, Triple, Quadruple) have a higher recommendation hit ratio, and double merging shows the best average hit rate. This proves that the proposed model performs better than other single algorithms.

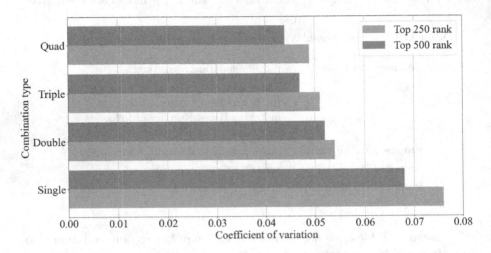

Fig. 4. Mean hit ratio of top 250 & top 500 by used recommendation algorithms.

To adequately compare our proposed model, we calculated each combination algorithm's coefficient of variation (CV). If the CV value is smaller, the recommendation effect of this algorithm is efficient. We can see from Fig. 4 that the CV values of the three combined types of the proposed HRM model are lower than that of a single algorithm, with an average reduction of about 28%.

4   Conclusion

As more and more people join the social network, a recommendation system that can make recommendations based on users' own characteristics can significantly improve the user experience. After analyzing the disadvantages of traditional recommendation systems, we propose a new recommendation model that integrates multiple recommendation algorithms. We use different combinations of a single recommendation algorithm to achieve effective recommended results. These results in Figs. 3 and 4 demonstrate that the testing effect of two combinations is better than that of a single or three. The effect of pm and nf is efficiently improved, and the recommendation performances of the hybrid model are more stable.

In the future, this hybrid model can not only be used for user recommendation of social network platforms but also be implemented to some shopping websites, books, movies, and music in daily recommendation platforms, which is of great significance for improving user experience.

References

1. Gao, J., Zhang, C., Xu, Y., Luo, M., Niu, Z.: Hybrid microblog recommendation with heterogeneous features using deep neural network. Expert Syst. Appl. **167**, 114191 (2021)
2. Rasool, A., Tao, R., Kamyab, M., Hayat, S.: GAWA-a feature selection method for hybrid sentiment classification. IEEE Access **8**, 191850–191861 (2020). https://doi.org/10.1109/ACCESS.2020.3030642
3. Rasool, A., Jiang, Q., Qu, Q., Ji, C.: WRS: a novel word-embedding method for real-time sentiment with integrated LSTM-CNN model. In: IEEE International Conference on Real-time Computing and Robotics (RCAR) 2021, pp. 590–595 (2021). https://doi.org/10.1109/RCAR52367.2021.9517671
4. Li, H., Han, D.: A time-aware hybrid recommendation scheme combining content-based and collaborative filtering. Front. Comput. Sci. **15**(4), 1–3 (2021). https://doi.org/10.1007/s11704-020-0028-7
5. Song, X., et al.: A hybrid recommendation system for marine science observation data based on content and literature filtering. Sensors **20**, 6414 (2020)
6. Kumaran, P., Chitrakala, S.: Topic adaptive sentiment classification based community detection for social influential gauging in online social networks. Multimed Tools Appl (2022). https://doi.org/10.1007/s11042-021-11855-3
7. Huang, M., Jiang, Q., Qu, Q., Rasool, A.: An overlapping community detection approach in ego-splitting networks using symmetric nonnegative matrix factorization. Symmetry **13**(5), 869 (2021)
8. Pérez-Almaguer, Y., Yera, R., Alzahrani, A.A., Martínez, L.: Content-based group recommender systems: a general taxonomy and further improvements. Expert Syst. Appl. **184**, 115444 (2021)
9. Sharma, S., Rana, V., Malhotra, M.: Automatic recommendation system based on hybrid filtering algorithm. Educ. Inf. Technol. **27**, 1523–1538 (2022)
10. Zhang, C., Duan, X., Liu, F., Li, X., Liu, S.: Three-way Naive Bayesian collaborative filtering recommendation model for smart city. Sustain. Urban Areas **76**, 103373 (2022)
11. Chen, J., Geyer, W., Dugan, C., Muller, M., Guy, I.: "Make new friends, but keep the old" - recommending people on social networking sites, vol. 10 (2009)
12. Ding, Y., Yan, E., Frazho, A., Caverlee, J.: PageRank for ranking authors in co-citation networks. J. Am. Soc. Inf. Sci. **60**, 2229–2243 (2009)
13. Golder, S.A., Yardi, S.: A structural approach to contact recommendations in online social networks, vol. 4 (2009)
14. Chen, L., et al.: Friendship prediction model based on factor graphs integrating geographical location. CAAI Trans. Intell. Technol. **5**, 193–199 (2020)
15. Yu, S.J.: The dynamic competitive recommendation algorithm in social network services. Inf. Sci. **187**, 1–14 (2012)
16. Open Twitter Dataset: http://an.kaist.ac.kr/traces/WWW2010.html. Accessed 29 Oct 2022

Author Index

Printed in the United States
by Baker & Taylor Publisher Services

Printed in the United States
by Baker & Taylor Publisher Services